TOWARDS THE DEATH OF SATAN

And the dragon fought and his angels, and prevailed not; neither was their place found any more in heaven. And the great dragon was cast out, that old serpent, called the devil, and Satan, which deceiveth the whole world.
Rev. 12, 7–9

For Rea

TOWARDS THE DEATH OF SATAN

The Growth and Decline
of
Christian Demonology

by

HENRY ANSGAR KELLY

GEOFFREY CHAPMAN
LONDON DUBLIN MELBOURNE 1968

Geoffrey Chapman Ltd
18 High Street, Wimbledon, London SW 19

Geoffrey Chapman (Ireland) Ltd
5-7 Main Street, Blackrock, County Dublin

Geoffrey Chapman Pty Ltd
44 Latrobe Street, Melbourne, Vic 3000, Australia

First published 1968

CONTENTS

v

ABBREVIATIONS

ANF   The Ante-Nicene Fathers. New York 1890.
CSEL   Corpus scriptorum ecclesiasticorum latinorum.
ES   Heinrich Denziger, *Enchiridion symbolorum.* Ed. A. Schönmetzer.
         Barcelona 1963.
GCS   Die griechischen christlichen Schriftsteller der ersten Jahrhunderte.
Loeb   The Loeb Classical Library.
LTK   Lexikon für Theologie und Kirche. 2 ed. Freiburg 1957ff.
NPNF A Select Library of the Nicene and Post-Nicene Fathers. Grand
         Rapids 1955-56.
PG   J. P. Migne, Patrologia graeca.
PL   J. P. Migne, Patrologia latina.

The citations from the bible for the most part follow the Revised Standard
Version.

Some of the material in the present book appeared earlier in "Demonology
and Diabolical Temptation," *Thought* 40 (1965) 165-94.

PREFACE

Belief in the devil and the demons of Christian tradition will always have a substantial place in any history of the development of Christianity. But whether a doctrine on the existence, properties, and activities of evil spirits deserves a place in Christian theology is another question.

The present work reflects a considered judgment that, far from constituting an essential teaching of Christian revelation, demonology is an accidental feature that has produced, and is the product of, a number of serious aberrations in the understanding of revealed religion. The discussion that follows is therefore to be read in the light of the possibility or even the likelihood that the devil and demons—that is, the fallen angels of traditional belief —do not exist.

It would be going too far to say with certainty that such creatures do not exist, since anything that is not self-contradictory is possible. Furthermore, one cannot disprove the existence of something that by definition escapes the detection of the human senses in its essential nature. The most that can be said in such a case is that its reality is not proven.

In our study of the sources of the beliefs and practices of Christians regarding evil spirits, we shall be concerned chiefly with the elaborations characteristic of the Roman Catholic Church. But the material should interest members of all Christian denominations (especially the Church of England, in which a similar investigation was called for some years ago) and all students of religion, since many of the basic concepts are common to most confessional groups within Christianity. The Catholic will find it of particular significance to learn that the existence of the devil need not be regarded as a defined doctrine of the Church (contrary to what is generally taught in seminary textbooks). But all Christians will be concerned to see that the standard view of the pre-cosmic fall of Lucifer and his angels, such as we have it in Milton's *Paradise Lost,* is in fact

1

not in scripture at all but is a post-biblical mythic product that seems to have resulted from the quasi-gnostic speculations of Origen.

The notion of the devil found in Christianity did not arise primarily from a need to discover a principle of evil in the world, but from a series of misapprehensions about the content of scripture and the demands it supposedly made upon the faith of the followers of Christ. Once these historical mistakes have been recognized, it will be possible to view with greater equanimity the implications of a demonless Christianity, both in itself and in its effect upon other religious concerns, as for example the questions of original sin and eternal punishment.

We will first trace the development of various themes in the Old and New Testaments which served as a basis for the later Christian systematization of demon-lore. Then we will turn to the actual development of these notions in the writings of the Fathers and in the early liturgical practices. Next we will take up three primary manifestations or consequences of the demonological doctrines, namely witchcraft, possession, and temptation. Even though these concepts often coincided in time in their evolution and application, we can consider them in the order named, for purposes of analysis. We should then be able to make some practical conclusions on the role that evil spirits have in present-day Christianity and on their prospects for the future.

I
BIBLICAL
BACKGROUND

1. The Monsters of the Old Testament

In the traditions of almost all primitive cultures we find an abundance of malevolent invisible beings thought to be responsible for the various ills and tribulations of life. It is therefore an indication of the sophistication of the Hebrew religion in its official form that very little of this perspective is evident in the writings of the Old Testament.

There were, however, two literary factors at work which gave rise to imagery that might be termed demonic, or that readily lent itself to incorporation into a system of demonology. These were the use of personification and the borrowing of names and concepts from surrounding pagan cults.

Personification was easily applied to disease and other causes of death. We read, for instance, in the psalms: "You will not fear . . . the pestilence that stalks in darkness, nor the destruction that wastes at noonday" (Ps. 91, 5-6). Death itself is often depicted as a ravening monster or a terrible hunter of human lives. The same role is given to Sheol, the underworld of the dead, or to the watery abyss (Tehom) beneath Sheol, or to *belial,* the state of loss or complete spoliation of goods that follows upon death. The psalmist at one point says, "The cords of Death encompassed me, the torrents of Perdition (*Belial*) assailed me; the cords of Sheol entangled me, the snares of Death confronted me" (18, 4-5), and elsewhere wicked men are called "sons of Belial" (1 Sam. 2, 12). Belial later became the most common name of the Prince of Darkness in the writings of the apocalyptic sect at Qumran; he corresponds in many ways to the Satan of the New Testament.

Sometimes it appears as if passions have been personified, like the spirit of fornication in Hosea (4, 12), or the spirit of discord that God sends to stir up trouble between Abimelech and the men of Shechem (Jg. 9, 23), or the spirit of ill-will from God that comes upon Saul (1 Sam. 18, 10). It may be, however, that such "spirits" were conceived of as real invisible beings whose function it was (usually upon a direct commission from God) to exercise men in various ways. As we shall see, these divine emissaries were not regarded as evil in themselves.

The other literary feature which we singled out, that of adopting elements from writings or traditions of other cultures, sometimes seems to reflect only the kind of decorative instinct indulged in by Christian poets when making allusions to classical mythology. At other times, of course, it may indicate that the author (or the people in general) really believed in some element of paganism that had been imperfectly assimilated into the Hebrew religion. It is often difficult to decide which of these alternatives is the more likely.

Isaiah, for instance, populates his desert scenes not only with hyenas, jackals, and similar beasts, but with Lilith (Is. 34, 14), who seems to have been a Babylonian she-demon, and with "hairy beings" (*seirim*), a word often translated as "satyrs" in English, since elsewhere the people are blamed for offering sacrifices to them (Lev. 17, 7; 2 Chr. 11, 15). Lefèvre suggests too that the personified diseases may have been influenced by Babylonian conceptions:

An example is Pazuzu, the southwest wind which carries malaria: on top of a naked, exaggeratedly thin body is a monstrous head with goat's horns on the forehead. Four wings and the claws of a beast of prey indicate the speed with which it dives down on its victim, plunging sharp nails into his flesh. "I am Pazuzu, son of Hanpa," says the inscription, "king of the evil spirits of the air. I swoop with violence from the mountains, spreading fever as I go." [1]

[1] A. Lefèvre, "Angel or Monster? The Power of Evil in the Old Testament," *Satan* (New York 1952) 54.

The great sea-monsters like Leviathan and Tannin (dragon) which Isaiah uses to symbolize Egypt (Is. 27, 1) and which the psalmist associates with God's feats of creation and redemption (Ps. 74, 13-14) are found under the same names and with the same characteristics in the writings of the North Semitic polytheistic system that antedated the Hebrew religion in Canaan.[2] There are other passages in the Old Testament which are clearly inspired by the accounts of quarrels among the gods of Canaanite mythology. Psalm 82, for instance, has preserved its heathen antecedents to the extent that God is portrayed as threatening to make the other gods mortal because they have been guilty of injustice. In a better known passage, Isaiah draws upon similar Ugaritic material to liken the overthrow of a current tyrant to the fall of *Helel ben Shahar,* "Daystar, son of Dawn" (in Latin, "Lucifer, qui mane oriebaris": Is. 14, 12). It was only in Christian times, beginning with Origen, that this imagery was applied allegorically to Satan. In the New Testament (2 Pet. 1, 19; Rev. 22, 16) it is Christ who is called the *lucifer* or morning star, a characterization that is continued in the ancient *Exultet* prayer of the Easter vigil liturgy.

2. The Rise of the Satan

In the early stages of the development of monotheism among the Israelites, the alien gods encountered in Israel's contacts with other peoples were as a rule not denied existence. But they were reinterpreted as "sons of God" on an angelic level, that is, members of the divine council of Yahweh, who from their subordinate position assisted him in ruling the universe. It is in this context that "the satan" of Job must be understood; he is no fallen spirit but a being with the same standing as the other sons of God who present themselves before Yahweh (Job 1, 6). The word *satan* is a common noun here; it has the fundamental meaning of "adversary," and is used of human beings as well as of spirits, usually to refer to an opposition arranged or sanctioned by God against

[2] See C. F. A. Shaeffer *Ugaritica* II (Mission de Ras Shamra 5, Paris 1949) 37. 46.

men. The earliest application of the word to a spiritual—that is, non-human or supernatural—agency occurs in the book of Numbers. Here we read in the Hebrew text that the *malak* (in Greek, *angelos* or messenger) of Yahweh, that is, Yahweh himself, tells Balaam that because he has proceeded against his will, he has come as a satan against him (Num. 22, 22. 32).

In the second book of Samuel it is recorded that the anger of Yahweh became kindled against Israel and caused David to number his subjects, thereby laying the nation open to divine punishment (2 Sam. 24, 1). But when the episode is retold in the first book of Chronicles, the author falls in with a tendency observable elsewhere in Jewish thought, namely, to stress God's transcendence above mundane activity, especially if it involved deeds that could be construed as not meeting the highest moral standards. He therefore says that it was "a satan" or even "Satan" (that is, he may mean it as a proper name) who urged David to take the census (1 Chr. 21, 1). It is not possible to determine whether the satan is considered evil here—that is, as unjustly opposed to David (or to God). There is no reason to suppose that such is the case, but it is easy to see how a figure of this sort could come to be regarded as evil. Already in the book of Job the satan is portrayed as cynical and skeptical of the virtue of men and as almost unethical in his efforts to expose what he considers to be the fair-weather quality of Job's uprightness.

In the pre-Christian Alexandrian rendition of the Old Testament into Greek (the Septuagint), the satans of Job and Chronicles, as well as the one who appears in Zechariah as a prosecuting attorney against the just priest Joshua (Zech. 3, 1-2), are translated as *ho diabolos,* "the devil" (from the verb *diaballein,* "to oppose"), a word that can mean "slanderer" as well as "adversary." In the book of Wisdom, a late work appearing only in the Septuagint, we read that a *diabolos* or adversary who was motivated by envy first brought death into the world (Wis. 2, 24). The *diabolos* referred to here may be the serpent in the garden of Eden or the envious Cain, who committed the first murder. The latter interpretation was the one adopted by Clement of Rome in the first century in his letter to the Corinthians (3-4). But it may also refer to a suprahuman being whose ill-will brought mankind to grief. The text was certainly interpreted in this way, eventually, at least, when it was caught up in the movement to attribute all evils to the instigation of a "satanic" spirit. Illustrations of the process can be found not only in the bible but also and more especially in apocryphal and rabbinical literature.

It became common to suppose that such a spirit entered the garden of Eden, not on a divine commission, but for his own purposes, and made use of the serpent, or even took on the form of a serpent, in order to tempt Eve. And the same spirit, or one similar to him, figures in many accounts of subsequent Old Testament episodes, including the story of Cain and Abel. The New Testament seems to reflect some of these notions when it speaks of the devil as a sinner, a liar, and a murderer from the beginning, and of Cain and other sinners as children of the devil (Jn. 8, 44; 1 Jn. 3, 8-12). But more precisely these passages seem to refer to the rabbinical interpretation of the Genesis account of the birth of Cain (Gen. 4, 1), where the name Cain (*Qayin*) is explained by Eve, who says she has acquired (*qanah*) a man with (the help of) Yahweh. The rabbis substituted Satan for Yahweh,[3] just as the chronicler did in the matter of David's impulse to take a census. In this view, therefore, Satan was regarded as the natural father of Cain. As we shall see, there was another much more prominent tradition that considered it possible for angels to beget children upon human females.

In his appearances as tempter, the satan just as often fails as succeeds. Job, of course, is the prime scriptural example of the upright man whose faith remains unshaken when tested by the satan, but in para-biblical literature Abraham is constantly portrayed as enduring the same process. According to Genesis it was God who tempted Abraham by commanding him to sacrifice his son (Gen. 22, 1), but the later interpretations usually attribute the idea for the trial to the suggestion of a satanic assistant.

3. The Temptation of Jesus

In a particularly interesting work of the later first century A.D.

[3] See Nils Alstrup Dahl, "Der Erstgeborene Satans und der Vater des Teufels," *Apophoreta* (Festschrift für Ernst Haenchen, Berlin 1964) 70-84.

known as *The Apocalypse of Abraham* there is a temptation of
Abraham near the beginning of his "public life" which resembles
Mark's account of Christ's temptation in the desert.[4] There
are other striking literary parallels to all three synoptic versions
of Christ's temptation by the devil, even apart from the obvious
analogy to the Old Testament accounts of the trials of the Israelites in the desert. For instance, Satan is sometimes portrayed as en-
gaging Abraham in a scriptural dispute in his effort to dissuade
him from sacrificing Isaac. This argumentative feature is also observable in stories of Moses and the angel of death (whose
role is sometimes played by the devil). In one account, the angel
of death quotes the psalms, and Moses answers each of his three
attempts by citing Deuteronomy,[5] a pattern followed by the devil
and Christ in the temptations described in Matthew and Luke.[6] We
might note that one version of the devil's disputatious attempt to
secure the body of Moses is recorded in the New Testament (Jude
9). Here the author commends the archangel Michael for not in-
sulting the devil; instead he asks God to pass judgment in the matter and rebuke his opponent, just as the angel of Yahweh did
in Zechariah (Zech. 3, 2). This passage in Jude is a borrowing
from an apocryphal work called *The Assumption of Moses.*[7]

Some commentators have remarked that aside from the temptations in the desert the opposition that Christ meets with in his
public life is due to the direct activity of human adversaries, even
though these persons are often linked to the devil in some way.
And it has been suggested [8] that since the temptation in the desert was not a witnessed event, as the gospel episodes purport to
be, the accounts of Matthew and Luke are a dramatic theological
expansion of events recorded elsewhere in the gospels, especially
three closely related episodes in John (Jn. 6-7). We read there
that Jesus fled an offered kingship, that on the next day he rebuked the people's implicit desire for more bread, and that his

[4] *The Apocalypse of Abraham* (ed. **G. H. Box,** London 1919) 43-55; cf.
Mk. 1, 9-13.
[5] *Deuteronomy Rabbah* 11, 5 (*Midrash Rabbah* 7, tr. J. Rabbinowitz, London 1961) 176.
[6] In Mt. 4, 1-11 and Lk. 4, 1-13 the devil quotes Ps. 91, 11-12, and Christ
responds to the temptations by citing Deut. 8, 3; 6, 16; and 6, 13.
[7] See R. H. Charles, *The Assumption of Moses* (London 1897) 105-10.
[8] By R. E. Brown, *New Testament Essays* (Milwaukee 1965) 203-07.

relatives urged him to go to Judea for the feast of tabernacles to manifest his works. This hypothesis of the non-historical, or metahistorical, character of the temptation in the desert is further strengthened by the presence of formal elements and literary conventions in the account, some of which we have just seen.[9]

4. Other New Testament Themes

In our history of the satan we saw that after he had become involved in unsavory employments, he began to be considered reprehensible for them. And once wickedness or guilt was ascribed to him, the next logical step would be to assign him a reckoning and punishment. Furthermore, it became a characteristic of the coming messianic age and of times of peace that the satan was put out of the way. This last point is illustrated several times in the early apocryphon of *Jubilees*,[10] where on one occasion Mastema (another form of the word *satan*) may be referring to his own future judgment (10, 8). These developments are perhaps best shown in the New Testament itself, where we see that Jesus has come to cast out "the ruler of this world" (Jn. 12, 31; cf. Rev. 12, 10); and according to the Apocalypse the devil will be bound for a time in the abyss of fire and then eventually cast forever into the lake of fire and brimstone (Rev. 20, 2-10).

By the time of the Christian era, stories about fallen angels had evolved, but the only account of such a fall in the New Testament is in the epistles of Jude and 2 Peter. According to this version, which is taken from the pseudepigraphous *Book of Enoch*,[11] a number of the angels lusted after the daughters of men before the flood and sinned with them. As a punishment they were chained in dark caves, to be kept in this state of imprisonment until judgment day, when they were to be consigned to the abyss of fire (Jude 6; 2 Pet. 2, 4). Thus they were not allowed to commit further evil among men. The earliest appearance of this story,

---

[9] For more details, see H. A. Kelly, "The Devil in the Desert," *Catholic Biblical Quarterly* 26 (1964) 190-220.
[10] *Jub.* 23, 29; 40, 9; 46, 2; 50, 5; in R. H. Charles, *The Apocrypha and Pseudepigrapha of the Old Testament* (Oxford 1963-4) II 49ff.
[11] *1 Enoch*, 10,4-5 and *passim* (Charles, *Apoc and Pseud.* II 193 etc.).

which is a commentary on an obscure episode in Genesis (Gen. 6, 1-4), seems to have been in an ancient *Book of Noah* (dated before 166 B.C.), fragments of which have been preserved in the *Book of Enoch*. It has a number of striking similarities to Greek mythology, to which it may be indebted.[12] Almost all the early Fathers of the Church accepted this view of the angels' fall through lust, though they believed the devil first fell (sinned) in tempting Eve. Origen appears to be the first to suggest a fall before man came onto the scene.

In the New Testament, there is no indication as to the origin of Satan; his fall "like lightning" in Luke (10, 18) and the fall of "the dragon and his angels" in the Apocalypse (12, 7-9) refer, as appears from their contexts, to the messianic or eschatological overthrow of Satan, and not to any primordial sin and punishment of the angels. The reference that Christ makes to the fire prepared for the devil and his angels in Matthew 25, 41 may of course be read as referring to the punishment to be undergone by the devil for his crimes against mankind; but it may also be interpreted to mean that the devil and his angels are placed in charge of the fiery torments and will act as the executors of the punishments of wicked men, which is the meaning suggested in other texts.[13]

In spite of the fact that the devil is mentioned in the Matthew passage and in the Apocalypse together with "his angels," he is always portrayed as a unique being in the New Testament, and he does not seem to be regarded simply as "first among equals." Moreover, he is not depicted as a fallen and punished angel, but as the ruler of the world, whose reign must give way to that of Christ.[14] In the Apocalypse, Satan appears in his Old Testament position in heaven, where he brings accusations night and day

---

[12] Cf. T. F. Glasson, *Greek Influence in Jewish Eschatology, with Special Reference to the Apocalypses and Pseudepigraphs* (London 1961) 62ff. For these and other possible foreign influences on the development of Jewish angelology and demonology, see D. S. Russell, *The Method and Message of Jewish Apocalyptic, 200 B.C.-A.D. 100* (London 1964) 257-62. An Iranian impetus seems especially likely.

[13] Cf. 1 Cor. 5, 5; 1 Tim. 1, 20; 3, 6; *1 Enoch* 53, 3; *Damascus Document* A 8, 2, in A. Dupont-Summer, *The Essene Writings from Qumran* (tr. G. Vermes, Cleveland 1962).

[14] For Satan as ruler of the world, see Kelly, "Devil in the Desert" 210-11.

against the Christians (Rev. 12, 10) until his eventual expulsion by Michael and his angels. Here too Satan is described with attributes of such primitive chaos-monsters as Rahab and Leviathan, which were no doubt associated with him because of their role in Job,[15] and perhaps also because of their prophetic connection with the world powers opposed to Israel. We saw above that Isaiah compared Egypt to Leviathan and the dragon, and in the book of Daniel four great beasts that come out of the sea represent successive reigning empires; in the Apocalypse the same kind of imagery is applied to the Roman dominion.

There is, then, only one devil in the New Testament, and he is looked upon as the author or instigator of evil for mankind, both moral and physical. He not only entices men to do wrong, but also seems to have control over diseases (Acts 10, 38) and to direct the unclean spirits or demons.[16]

These unclean possessing spirits, which receive treatment only from the synoptic writers, are mysterious beings. They are difficult to connect with any of the Jewish traditions, except in some stray details. Their origin is never hinted at; they show no affinity to the fallen angels of *1 Enoch,* and little resemblance even to the evil spirits that issued from the bodies of the giants, who themselves were the offspring of the union between the angels and the daughters of men. However, the accounts of the Gerasene demoniac manifest a belief, at least on the part of the demoniac (or "Legion"), that the possessing demons are to suffer a fate similar to that of the spirits of the giants, by being cast into "the abyss" (Mt. 8, 29; Lk. 8, 31).

The gospel demons have none of the characteristics of the devil himself, except perhaps for their knowledge of or interest in the Messiah. Unlike the devil and unlike the giant-ghosts, they are not tempters; they have no moral direction, but simply cause physical and mental disturbances by indwelling. This latter function in turn is not a characteristic of the devil. English bibles that speak of "driving out devils" are faultily translated.

[15] See Job. 3, 8; 9, 13; 41, 1ff.
[16] Lk. 10, 17-19; 13, 11-16; Mt. 12, 22-29; Mk. 3, 22-27.

5. The Demons of the Septuagint

The synoptic concept of disease demons may have been influenced by the Septuagint, which was familiar to the compilers of the New Testament. It is the Septuagint version of Psalm 91 that the devil quotes when tempting Jesus in the desert (Mt. 4, 6), and in the same psalm occurs the verse cited above as an example of personified disease, where "the destruction that wastes at noonday" becomes in the Greek "mischance and noonday demon." Similarly, the goats or satyrs (*seirim*) that inhabit Isaiah's wastelands along with other unclean beasts have become demons who will dance in the company of sirens in the ruins of Babylon (Is. 13, 21) and meet with the ass-centaurs [17] in Edom (Is. 34, 14), a land symbolizing the nations in league against Israel.

It is quite evident that these latter demons are visualized as living, visible, beast-like creatures and not as unseen spirits. We have seen that the people perversely offered sacrifice to *seirim* (Lev. 17, 7), and Jeroboam set up priests for the *seirim* and the calves that he had made (2 Chr. 11, 15). The Septuagint translates *seirim* in the latter passage as "idols and worthless things," and in the Leviticus verse simply as "worthless things" (*mataia*).

Elsewhere the process is reversed: Where the Hebrew text reads that all the gods (*elohim*) of the gentiles are worthless (*elilim*), the Greek, incapable of reproducing the pun, says that the gods (*theoi*) are demons (*daimonia*: Ps. 96, 5). In another psalm the Septuagint translates as demons the word *shedim,* which refers to the object of human sacrifice (Ps. 106, 37). *Shedim* were Assy-

---

[17] The ass-centaur is described in a work on *The Red Sea* by Pythagoras, who wrote in Egypt in the 3rd century B.C.; he is cited by Aelian in his treatise on *The Characteristics of Animals* (17, 9). This animal, as Aelian describes it, with head and front appendages like those of a man but with hind legs like those of an ass, has been taken to mean the gorilla or chimpanzee, although there is nothing particularly ass-like about these animals. It would seem to resemble more closely the classical picture of a satyr, half man and half goat. Aelian could have seen a picture of an ass-centaur in the great mosaic of the Nile in his home town of Praeneste, where the entire body, however, including the front legs are those of an ass; it is surmounted by a sphinx-like head of a woman. Aelian uses the feminine form of the word (*onokentaura*), which is also how it appears in the mosaic. See Giorgio Gullini, *I Mosaici di Palestrina,* (Rome 1956) Plate 26.

rian protective deities, especially the bull-colossi that guarded portals. St. Paul (1 Cor. 10, 20) cites a similar passage from Deuteronomy, where the people are accused of sacrificing to *shedim* and not to God (32, 17). But though Paul uses the Septuagint translation of *daimonia,* it is evident from his epistle that he thinks of these demons who received the worship of pagans as lifeless idols (1 Cor. 12, 2).

This understanding of demons in the prophetic sense of manufactured images is also found in the Septuagint, as is clearly illustrated in a passage of Isaiah condemning pagan rites (Is. 65, 3). The Greek specifies the object of the worship as "demons who do not exist"; that is, there are no spiritual entities corresponding to the idols. But when the first letter to Timothy warns against "spirits of error and teachings of demons" (4, 1), evil spirits of some sort may be meant, although the admonition seems to be aimed directly against men who are proponents of erroneous doctrines on sex and food. However, James is obviously thinking of living beings when he says in his letter that "even the demons believe and tremble" (2, 19). Similarly, in the Apocalypse there are demons in the sense of man-made idols (Rev. 9, 20) as well as living ones; the latter are unclean spirits like frogs that issue from the mouths of the dragon, the beast, and the false prophet (Rev. 16, 13-14). The most developed account of a demon in the scriptures, however, is that of the murderous demon Asmodeus in the book of Tobit, which appears only in the Septuagint and reflects the demonological speculations of the Jews in Egypt.

Another peculiarly Egyptian reference in the Septuagint can be found in the polemic of Isaiah against the worship of Gad, the god of fortune (Is. 65, 11). The Greek renders Gad by using "demon" in its masculine form (*daimon*), whereas in all other instances in the Septuagint the neuter form (*daimonion*) is employed; the translator is thereby protesting the Alexandrian cult of the Good Demon (*Agathos Daimon*).[18]

We may note here that rabbinical speculation in the Talmud and other commentaries developed several different accounts of the origin of demons. They were regarded "as unfortunate spirits

[18] See Siegfried Morenz, "Ägyptische Spuren in den Septuaginta," *Mullus* (Festschrift Theodor Klauser, Münster 1964) 251.

14

which were left bodiless when the Sabbath suddenly began on the sixth day of creation; as the builders of the tower of Babel who were transformed into demons as punishment; as metamorphosed male hyenas; or the offspring of illicit unions of Adam with female spirits and Eve with male spirits." [19] One account has it that the demons can reproduce themselves: "Like angels, they have wings and fly from one end of the world to the other, and know the future; and like men they eat, propagate, and die." [20] Although these traditions were not written down until well after the beginning of the Christian era, one or other of them may be of sufficient antiquity to have influenced the gospel demonology. Josephus, writing towards the end of the first century A.D., records a concept of demons that may have developed from the story of the spirits of the giants and is almost identical to the superstition of the *dibbuk* among modern Eastern European Jews. He says in the *Jewish War* that demons are "the spirits of wicked men which enter the living and kill them unless aid is forthcoming" (7, 185 Loeb).

6. The Principalities and Powers of St. Paul

The angelology of the Pauline epistles is also very important for later demonological developments. Paul inherited the Jewish view that angels (the principalities and powers) were delegated by God to rule the world. We recall that the Canaanite pantheon (consisting of nature deities) became incorporated into the Hebrew system as "sons of God," angelic members of the divine council. The same was true of the astral divinities of the East, who made up the heavenly hosts (*sabaoth*); Yahweh became the God of the *sabaoth*. The Septuagint sometimes translates this phrase as "Lord God of the powers" (as in Ps. 80, 4).

The book of Deuteronomy developed the function of the angels further when it stated that God divided men into nations "according to the number of the angels of God" (Septuagint reading), so

---

[19] S. Vernon McCasland, *By the Finger of God; Demon Possession and Exorcism in Early Christianity in the Light of Modern Views of Mental Illness* (New York 1951) 75-76.
[20] See Kaufman Kohler, "Demonology," *Jewish Encyclopedia,* 4, 517.

that each nation would have its angelic ruler, except Israel, which was ruled directly by Yahweh himself (Dt. 32, 8-9). Since these angels had their authority from God, they commanded respect and obedience, but, like the human rulers under them, they could be delinquent or unjust in fulfilling their duties. We have seen that in Psalm 82 Yahweh threatens to punish the "gods" for their failure to rule justly; and in apocalyptic passages in Isaiah (24, 21; 34, 2-4) it is prophesied that the angelic powers of the rebellious nations will be defeated and punished along with their earthly kings and people.

St. Paul extended the concept of the angelic rule of the nations to include authority over astrological and natural forces and also over the Mosaic law.[21] As for Satan, he is sometimes viewed as a law-enforcer or a source of salutary affliction. For instance, the man guilty of incest is to be delivered over to Satan to punish his flesh so that his spirit might be saved (1 Cor. 5, 5), and Paul himself refers to his own bodily ailment as an angel of Satan which was given to him to keep him from pride (2 Cor. 12, 7). But the devil is also closely associated with the principalities and powers in their role as rulers of the universe, especially in the letter to the Ephesians (6, 11-16). Similarly, the dragon-devil in the Apocalypse, apart from his function of accuser in heaven, appears to be regarded as the power behind the Roman empire, as does Belial in the Dead Sea scrolls.

The passage from Ephesians just referred to emphasizes that the devil and the powers are regarded as the source of obstacles and temptations that Christians must constantly guard against. But if their authority over the Jewish law and nature (Col. 2; Gal. 4) and even over the state (1 Cor. 2, 6-8; 6, 3) has been largely superseded by the coming of Christ, they still command some deference (1 Cor. 11, 10-11) and obedience (Rom. 13, 1-6) because they function as God's ministers, in spite of their capacity for evil.

Paul's own career eventually taught him to admire the workings of the Roman state, at whose hands he demanded and received justice. G. B. Caird sums up the corresponding development in the apostle's attitude toward the angelic rulers:

[21] On these points see especially G. B. Caird, *Principalities and Powers; a Study in Pauline Theology* (Oxford 1956).

In his earlier writings Paul accepted the apocalyptic outlook,
which did not look beyond the defeat of those spiritual powers which were at enmity with God. They belonged to the
present age, and with the passing of the present age they too
would pass away. But in his imprisonment epistles he has be-
gun to entertain the hope that even the powers may be
brought within the scope of God's redemption. God had exalted Christ "that at the name of Jesus every knee should
bow, of those in heaven and those on earth and those under
the earth, and that every tongue should confess that Jesus
Christ is Lord" (Phil. 2, 10-11). The heavenly powers are
among those who must come to acknowledge the lordship of
Christ, for it was to this end that they were created. Christ is
"the firstborn of all creation, because in him all things were
created in heaven and on earth, visible and invisible, whether
thrones or lordships or principalities or authorities; . . . in
him all the fullness of God was pleased to dwell, and through
him to reconcile to himself all things, whether on earth or in
heaven, making peace by the blood of his cross" (Col. 1, 16-
20). Nor is this some far-off, divine event, to take place in the
twinkling of an eye, at the last trumpet: it is happening now.
For it is God's purpose "that to the principalities and authorities in the heavenly places there might now be made known
through the church the manifold wisdom of God" (Eph. 3,
10). Like the redemption of the Christian, the redemption of
the powers is achieved by the cross, worked out in the present, and consummated at the *parousia*.[22]

Caird admits that "the hope that the powers will be reconciled to
God is thrown out without any elaboration, so that we are left to
conjecture what such a hope involves."[23] The important thing, however, is to recognize that Paul could arrive at such a hope of reform
and redemption for angels who strayed from doing the will of God.
It was the apocalyptic outlook (as Caird terms it) that was to pre-
vail in later thought, so much so that by late patristic and medieval
times it became impossible to think of angels in the world of men

[22] Caird, *Principalities* 27-28.
[23] *Ibid.* 83.

except as either totally good and incapable of sin, or as thoroughly evil and irrevocably doomed to remain so until their final and everlasting incarceration in a place of torture.

This brief survey of biblical themes related to what has become known as demonology reveals the great disparity of source materials and concepts that exists in the scriptures. There is no systematic demonology present; that comes only later, and only at the cost of distorting the biblical data to Procrustean specifications. A common factor behind the biblical motifs is the need to describe intelligibly the cause of obstacles to human happiness. But the explanations are invariably flavored by notions inherited or borrowed from cultures alien to Judaism. The same process, of course, is at work in post-biblical developments, to which we now turn.

II
THE ELABORATIONS OF
THE FATHERS

1. Jewish Apocalyptic and Jewish Christianity

The speculations concerning the spirit world that we have traced in the bible were produced by the Jewish mentality, however much they may have been influenced by Babylonian and other cults from the East and Greek philosophy from the West. It is natural, then, to look for the earliest Christian interpretations of the biblical material in the community of Jewish Christians.[1]

The early Jewish converts to Christianity drew heavily upon apocalyptic tracts compiled by sects on the fringes of Judaism. Most of these writings, which are usually grouped under the title of "pseudepigrapha of the Old Testament," are filled with interpolations from Christian editors, and even original Jewish-Christian compositions rely extensively upon these purely Jewish works. An example can be found in the canonical epistle of Jude, which is itself a pseudepigraphous work (that is, the author, a Jewish-Christian of the second century, falsely claims to be the apostle Jude).

---

[1] Unfortunately, Jewish and Jewish-Christian angelology and demonology have often received very inadequate treatment in recent works. For instance, Jean Daniélou in *The Theology of Jewish Christianity* (tr. and ed. John A. Baker, London 1964) seriously misconstrues the nature of the guardian angels of the nations by considering them to be identified with the angels who sinned with women; Bo Reicke in *The Disobedient Spirits and Christian Baptism; a Study of 1 Pet 3, 19 and Its Context* (Copenhagen 1946) and in *The Epistles of James, Peter, and Jude* (Anchor Bible, Garden City 1964) seems to be completely unfamiliar with the tradition of the angelic guardians; and Heinrich Schlier in *Principalities and Powers in the New Testament* (New York 1961) is prevented from arriving at the real nature of the principalities and powers because of dogmatic and theological commitments to the later Christian conception of fallen angels. William J. Dalton, *Christ's Proclamation to the Spirits* (Analecta biblica 23, Rome 1965), has inherited all of these weaknesses.

As we have seen in the first chapter, Jude 6 draws on *1 Enoch* for its account of the fall of the angels, and Jude 9 cites from *The Assumption of Moses* the story of the quarrel between Michael and the devil over the body of Moses.

The *Book of Enoch* is unquestionably the most important of the pseudepigrapha, and it will be worthwhile to review some of its angelological and demonological elements at length. We have already discussed the story of the angels (called Watchers) who sinned with women and begot giants. God then condemned them by giving these instructions to Michael:

> Go, bind Semjaza and his associates who have united themselves with women so as to have defiled themselves with them in all their uncleanness. And when their sons have slain one another, and they have seen the destruction of their beloved ones, bind them fast for seventy generations in the valleys of the earth, till the day of their judgment and of their consummation, till the judgment that is for ever and ever is consummated. In those days they shall be led off to the abyss of fire, and to the torment and the prison in which they shall be confined for ever. And whosoever shall be condemned and destroyed will from thenceforth be bound together with them to the end of all generations. (10, 11-14)

These angels, therefore, after their initial dereliction of duty and a brief period of impunity on earth before the deluge, were permanently put out of action and could no longer interfere in earthly matters. After the giants were killed in internecine conflicts, however, evil spirits issued forth from their bodies; and these spirits, Enoch learns, "shall destroy without incurring judgment . . . until the day of the consummation, the great judgment in which the age shall be consummated, over the Watchers and the godless" (16, 1).

In another part of *1 Enoch* the story of the lustful Watchers is retold, but now they are allegorized as stars (86, 1-4). After they are cast into the abyss, the history of Israel is developed chronologically, but in allegorical form. During the period between the building of the Temple and its destruction, there occurs a version of the tradition of the seventy guardian angels, presented here under the guise of seventy shepherds. But instead of ruling the pagan nations, they are deputed to rule the Israelites, who are, of course, the sheep of the shepherds. We may perhaps find in this concept a clue to St. Paul's notion of the principalities and powers as mediators of the Mosaic law as well as rulers of the nations.

The seventy shepherds are commanded to slay a certain number of sheep and no more; God meanwhile authorizes another to tabulate the destruction that they cause over and above what he has commanded, so that he may eventually punish them for it (89, 59-65). At the time of the judgment before the resurrection of the righteous there will occur, and does occur in Enoch's dream-vision, the general judgment, in which condemnation will come upon the fallen angels ("the stars whose privy members were like those of horses"), the over-zealous guardian angels ("those seventy shepherds to whom I delivered the sheep, and who taking them on their own authority slew more than I commanded them") and the apostate Jews ("those blinded sheep": 90, 21-26).

We see here a good illustration of the apocalyptic temperament, a development of the theme from the late passages in Isaiah cited in the previous chapter. Another illustration is to be found in the Apocalypse itself, where the martyrs cry out to God not for the conversion of their enemies but for their punishment, in the spirit of the imprecatory psalms (Rev. 6, 10). We have also seen that, though St. Paul at first did not go beyond the apocalyptic vision of the punishment of wicked angels as well as men, he later arrived at a hope that they would eventually be reconciled with God. Justin and Origen were to come to a similar conclusion.

Satan does not appear in the ancient sections of *1 Enoch,* but is mentioned in the part known as the "Similitudes" or "Parables." Because this portion of the book has not been found in the ancient library of Qumran, it has been conjectured that it is of Jewish-Christian origin. Here, apart from the satans who attempt to bring accusations before God against earthdwellers (40, 7), Satan is pictured as being in charge of the tortures that the angels of punishment will inflict upon evil-doers, including the Watchers, who are said to have become subject to Satan when they became unrighteous and led men astray (53, 3—54, 6).

Later demonology will preserve the picture of Satan as the eschatological director of torments but will specify that he too simultaneously undergoes punishment. We suggested before that this idea might already be contained in the *Book of Jubilees* where, after God has ordered all the spirits of the giants to be bound, we read: "And the chief of the spirits, Mastema, came and said: 'Lord, Creator, let some of them remain before me, and let them hearken to my voice and do all that I shall say unto them; for if some of them are not left to me, I shall not be able to execute the power of my will on the sons of men; for these are for corruption and leading astray before my judgment, for great is the wickedness of the sons of men.' " (10, 8)

One of the evils with which the spirits became associated was idolatry. *Jubilees* tells of the men in the land of the Chaldees who "made for themselves molten images, and they worshipped each the idol, the molten image which they had made for themselves, and they began to make graven images and unclean simulacra, and malignant spirits assisted and seduced them into committing transgressions and uncleanness. And the prince Mastema exerted himself to do all this, and he sent forth other spirits, those which were put under his hand, to do all manner of wrong and sin and all manner of transgression, to corrupt and destroy and to shed blood upon the earth." (11, 4-5)

In a section of the *Book of Enoch* that R. H. Charles believes is dependent upon *Jubilees,* unclean spirits are specified as among the recipients of religious homage: judgment is threatened against those "who worship stones and grave images of gold and silver and wood and stone and clay and those who worship impure spirits and demons and all kinds of idols not according to knowledge." (99, 7)

In an early passage of *Enoch* Uriel says: "Here shall stand the angels who have connected themselves with women, and their spirits assuming many different forms are defiling mankind and shall lead them astray into sacrificing to demons [the Greek adds "as gods" to the Ethiopic text], here shall they stand, till the day of the great judgment in which they shall be judged till they are made an end of. And the women also of the angels who went astray shall become sirens." (19, 1-2) To be consistent with the rest of *Enoch* the "spirits" here would have to refer to the spirits of the giants; and since the giant-spirits are not referred to as demons elsewhere in the book, the demons spoken of here may have another meaning. We saw that in the Septuagint *daimonia* can designate either idols or imaginary gods or the fantastic creatures of the desert. But *Enoch* could also be interpreted to mean that the fallen angels themselves are somehow able to remain upon earth and to seduce men into worshipping their demon offspring. Such an interpretation offers a picture that corresponds in many ways to the views of Justin and his contemporaries.

2. The Demonology of Justin

Justin Martyr, the most significant of the second-century Greek apologists, was an especially important influence in spreading Jewish apocalyptic notions among Christians outside the Semitic world. Although he was not himself Jewish, he was a native of Samaria, and his conversion to Christianity came after he had become acquainted with Greek philosophy; he was therefore able to appeal to intellectual circles of both East and West on their own terms. But in the process of harmonizing his Hebraic and Hellenistic backgrounds and synthesizing the traditions inherited from each, he arrived at a demonology considerably different from the traditions found in earlier Jewish-Christian writings.

In the first place, he combined the concept of the angelic custodians of nature and mankind, which we have seen in St. Paul, with the story of the fall of the angels through sexual passion, which is not in Paul. He says in his *Second Apology*:

> God, when he had made the whole world, and subjected things earthly to man, and arranged the heavenly elements for the increase of fruits and rotation of the seasons, and appointed this divine law—for these things also he evidently made for man—committed the care of men and of all things under heaven to angels whom he appointed over them. But the angels transgressed this appointment, and were captivated by love of women, and begat children who are those that are called demons. (*2 Apol.* 5 ANF)

Justin merges the two kinds of delinquent angels. He does this, not by identifying the region inhabited by the principalities and powers—that is, the air or one of the heavens—with the location of the prison of the lustful angels,[2] but by ignoring the tradition that the angels who sinned with women in the time of Noah were punished and permanently removed from contact with mankind.

According to Justin, therefore, the angelic rulers of the universe first sinned out of love for women—that is, except for Satan, "the prince of the evil demons," who was the serpent that deceived Eve.[3] The endless punishment in store for Satan and his army and the men who follow him has been delayed for the sake of those men who will repent, some of whom have not yet been born (*1 Apol.* 28). But angels, too, are able to repent after sinning, for, he says,

> if the word of God foretells that some angels and men shall be certainly punished, it did so because it foreknew that they would be unchangeably wicked, but not because God had created them so. So that if they repent, all who wish for it can obtain mercy from God. (*Dialogue with Trypho* 141)

Satan is one of the angels whom God foresaw as unrepentant; his punishment, implicit in the curse uttered against him in Eden, will consist of ultimate defeat by Christ and condemnation to eternal fire. This fate was prophesied for him by Isaiah in a passage where, as we saw in the last chapter, Egypt is personified in the Canaanite dragons, Lotan (Leviathan) and Tannin. The oracle reads: "In that day the Lord with his hard and great and strong sword will punish Leviathan the fleeing serpent, Leviathan the twisting serpent, and he will slay the dragon (*Tannin*) that is in the sea" (Is. 27, 1). However, the catastrophe that the Old Testament

---

[2] Daniélou assumes that such a conception was present in earlier Jewish-Christian writings, including Paul's epistles (*Theol. of Jewish Christianity* 174. 187-90. 234-35), but none of the texts he cites justifies this assumption.

[3] *1 Apol.* 28; *Dialogue with Trypho* 45. 79. 124. This belief that Satan first sinned in leading Adam and Eve astray was shared by other Greek apologists, namely, Tatian and Theophilus. Athenagoras, on the other hand, considered that the fault of the angel who was the prince of matter was his neglect in carrying out the duties assigned to him. See Heinrich Wey, *Die Funktionen der bösen Geister bei den griechischen Apologeten des zweiten Jahrhunderts nach Christus* (Winterthur 1957) 3-97.

prophets predicted did not become clear to Satan until he heard the discourses of Christ and his apostles.[4]

Another important aspect of Justin's demonology is his analysis of the gods of Greek mythology in terms of fallen angels and demons. In proving to the Jew Trypho that the Old Testament speaks of sinful angels, he cites the Septuagint version of Psalm 96, 5, which states that "all the gods of the nations are demons" (*Dial.* 79). "Demons" for Justin does not have the Septuagint meaning of "idols," but, as is indicated in the passage cited above from the *Second Apology,* designates the children of the union between angels and the daughters of men. He does not allude to that part of the tradition that declared the angel offspring to be giants, from whose corpses the demons emerged, but rather he seems to visualize the demons as the immediate issue of the angels and as endowed with a nature like that of their angelic progenitors.

In the text just alluded to, Justin continues his explanation:

And besides, they afterwards subdued the human race to themselves, partly by magical writings, and partly by fears and the punishments they occasioned, and partly by teaching them to offer sacrifices and incense and libations, of which things they stood in need after they were enslaved by lustful passions; and among men they sowed murders, wars, adulteries, intemperate deeds, and all wickedness. Whence also the poets and mythologists, not knowing that it was the angels and those demons who had been begotten by them that did these things to men and women and cities and nations, which they related, ascribed them to god himself, and to those who were accounted to be his very offspring, and to the offspring of those who were called his brothers, Neptune and Pluto, and to the children again of these their offspring. For whatever name

[4] See *Dial.* 91. 112, and the quotation from Justin's lost polemic against Marcion preserved by Irenaeus, *Heresies* 5, 26. Another version of Justin's sentiments appears in the writings of John of Antioch and Oecumenius Triccensis, and gives the specific example of the "Lucifer" passage in Isaiah 14 as a prediction of the devil's eventual ruin. But J. C. T. Otto considers this version a paraphrase and not a direct quotation of Justin's words; see his *Corpus apologetarum christianorum saeculi secundi* 3 (ed. 3, Jena 1879) 252.

each of the angels had given to himself and his children, by that name they called them. (2 *Apol.* 5)

In addition to their activities as pagan gods, the demons are also responsible for possessing demoniacs and Justin lays great stress upon the power of Christians to effect cures where other exorcists have failed (2 *Apol.* 6; *Dial.* 30).

We have suggested before that the Jewish story of the fallen Watchers and their demon children was influenced by Greek mythology. If so, Justin brought the legend full circle by combining it with Greek traditions once more. His disparaging attitude toward demons, if not his Jewish-flavored account of their origin and nature, was in fact shared by certain pagan thinkers. Arthur Darby Nock attributes the lessened esteem for the minor gods, who were grouped under the name demons, to "an increasing trend to monotheism among thoughtful men, an aversion, less widespread but noticeable, from ordinary cult, and a very common reluctance to accept myth at its face value." He continues: "Celsus, Porphyry and other writers tell us that *daimones* induce us to believe that bloody sacrifices and incense offerings are necessary, their motive being a selfish desire to feed on them. By this means they make us corporeal and like themselves and distract us from the service of higher powers. Again, a tractate in the *Corpus hermeticum* states that *daimones* drive the evil to fresh sins (16, 10ff)." [5]

3. The Philosophies and Religions of Egypt

With Celsus and the Hermetic writings our attention shifts to Egypt. Alexandria, one of the most important centers of learning in the world at the beginning of the Christian era, exercised a massive influence upon the development of Christian demonology. It was the home of the Septuagint version of the bible, which, as we have seen, inspired a number of demonological concepts in the New Testament and in Justin. Here too Philo the Jew found philosophical and theological allegories in the Old Testament, just as

[5] A. D. Nock, *Conversion: the Old and the New in Religion from Alexander the Great to Augustine of Hippo* (Oxford 1933) 223-24.

Plutarch did in Egyptian myth, by applying the Stoic method of allegorizing Homer. We know next to nothing of the origins of Christianity in Egypt; St. Paul did not go there on his missionary journeys, and no apostolic Father lived there. But by the middle of the second century the Christian community was flourishing there, along with a gnosticism of heavily Christian orientation. Clement of Alexandria was the first important thinker produced by the Christian school at Alexandria, but it is Origen at the beginning of the third century who was to play the most decisive role in the sphere of demonology.

As Jean Daniélou points out in describing the intellectual background of Origen, the prevailing philosophy of the second century was middle Platonism, such as that expounded by Plutarch, and it is this system that most nearly approaches Origen's thought, with its peculiar version of the Platonic theory of the emanation, debasement, and eventual purification of being, and also its great emphasis upon demons as intermediaries between gods and men.[6]

Daniélou also stresses the importance of Platonism and its contact with Egyptian religion for the growth of the Valentinian gnosis and the Hermetic system, the latter being a form of gnostic thought without admixture of Christian elements.

The similarities between gnosticism and Origen's thought are particularly striking. There is disagreement about how and when the gnostic movement originated; some believe it to be essentially Jewish, while others claim a Christian basis, and still others find its origin in pagan thought, either Hellenistic or Oriental. One theory, for instance, holds that it was the result of the disappointed hopes of Jewish apocalyptic sects after the destruction of the Temple of Jerusalem in 70 A.D.[7] What is certain is that it freely made use of many elements, Jewish, Christian, and pagan, religious and philosophical. In fact, much of what St. Paul says about the angelic archons or rulers of this age could almost be characterized as gnostic, or at least protognostic.

There were many different gnostic sects, but Hans Jonas groups them into two basic categories: the Iranian, in which darkness co-

[6] J. Daniélou, *Origen* (tr. W. Mitchell, New York 1955) 85-89.
[7] Robert M. Grant, *La gnose et les origines chrétiennes* (rev. ed. of *Gnosticism and Early Christianity,* tr. J. H. Marrou, Paris 1964) 31-38; cf. Preface by H. I. Marrou, 8-9.

exists with divine light from the beginning; and the Syrian-Egyptian type, which starts only with the divine light, and the world of darkness and evil is somehow generated from it.[8] It is, of course, the second form that was prevalent in Origen's culture.

According to the general gnostic view, "the world is the work of lowly powers which, though they may be mediately descended from him, do not know the true God and obstruct the knowledge of him in the cosmos over which they rule. The genesis of these lower powers, the archons (rulers), and in general that of all the orders of being outside God, including the world itself, is a main theme of gnostic speculation." The tyrannical world-rule of the archons is the all-encompassing Fate of astrological excogitation. "In its physical aspect this rule is the law of nature; in its psychical aspect, which includes for instance the institution and enforcement of the Mosaic Law, it aims at the enslavement of man. As guardian of his sphere, each archon bars the passage to the souls that seek to ascend after death, in order to prevent their escape from the world and their return to God." [9]

The word *gnosis* means "knowledge," and refers to the revelation necessary for men to be saved, which is imparted by a transcendent savior. On its practical side, the gnosis consists of "the sacramental and magical preparations for its future ascent and the secret names and formulas that force the passage through each sphere" and the archon who guards it.[10] But demonic forces must be combated in this life as well as in the next. As we shall see, the initiation-liturgy of one form of gnosticism in Egypt, that described by Theodotus, incorporated Christian baptism and accompanied it with elaborate methods of expelling and escaping unclean spirits and evil principalities. Finally, at least according to some systems, all the elements of divinity in the cosmos, archons as well as men, will be retrieved, and the realm of darkness, that is, the cosmos itself, will come to an end.

[8] H. Jonas, *The Gnostic Religion; the Message of the Alien God and the Beginnings of Christianity* (Boston 1963) 130.
[9] *Ibid.* 42-43.
[10] *Ibid.* 45.

4. Origen's Cosmic Speculations

One of the most brilliant thinkers in the history of Christianity, Origen could not but be deeply influenced by the philosophical and religious currents of his day, even as he sought to oppose their more obvious errors. It is often difficult to determine precisely what his true views were, since his most important speculations do not exist in their original Greek, but in doctored translations and biased reports made by later partisans or opponents of his thought. To make matters more complicated, Origen often merely suggests theories as possible explanations of scriptural data, historical events, or ontological circumstances, and at times his various suggestions contradict each other. But in the general lines of his world-view that emerge from his writings one can readily see similarities with both Platonic emanation theories and gnostic creation myths.

A cardinal tenet of Origen's system is that all beings endowed with intelligence—including, therefore, angels, men, and evil spirits—were created at the same time and with the same nature before the material world existed. Even in the translation of the *De principiis* made by Rufinus, the champion of Origen's orthodoxy, we can find this view elaborated:

When [God] in the beginning created those beings which he desired to create, that is, rational creatures, he had no other reason for creating them than on account of himself, that is, his own goodness. As he himself, then, was the cause of the existence of those things which were to be created, in whom there was neither any variation nor change, nor want of power, he created all whom he made equal and alike, because there was in himself no reason for producing variety and diversity. But since those rational creatures themselves. . . were endowed with the power of free will, this freedom of will incited each one either to progress by imitation of God. or reduced him to failure through negligence. And this, as we have already stated, is the cause of the diversity among rational creatures, deriving its origin not from the will or judgment of the creator, but from the freedom of the individual will. (2,9,6 ANF)

This paragraph as it now reads does not accurately reproduce Origen's complete theory as we can find it expressed elsewhere; in particular, he does not believe that any of the rational creatures he describes progressed from their original state to a more perfect one, but rather he holds that every one of these intelligences, except for Christ, was delinquent to some degree, even those who became "good" angels. We see a statement to this effect earlier in Rufinus' translation: "Each understanding (*mens*), neglecting goodness either to a greater or more limited extent, was dragged into the opposite of good, which undoubtedly is evil" (2,9,2).

He can find certain details about this primordial fall by a close reading of scripture. He knows, for instance, that "what is said in many places, and especially in Isaiah, of Nebuchadnezzar, cannot be explained of that individual. For the man Nebuchadnezzar neither fell from heaven, nor was he the morning star, nor did he arise upon the earth in the morning" (4,3,9 = 4,1,23). Isaiah 14 therefore refers to the devil: "Most evidently by these words is he shown to have fallen from heaven, who formerly was Lucifer (morning star), and who used to arise in the morning. . . . Nay, even the Savior himself teaches us, saying of the devil, 'Behold, I see Satan fallen from heaven like lightning' " (1,5,5).

But just as the diversity of rational beings was caused by a turning away from God at the beginning, Origen believes that the process will eventually be reversed and that all will regain their original status: "We think, indeed, that the goodness of God, through his Christ, may recall all his creatures to one end, even his enemies being conquered and subdued" (1,6,1). Johannes Quasten says of this surmise:

It is a grand vision, according to which the souls of those who have committed sins here on earth will be submitted to a purifying fire after death, whereas the good ones will enter paradise, that is, a kind of school in which God will solve all problems of the world. Origen does not know any eternal fire or punishment of hell. All sinners will be saved, even the de-

mons and Satan himself will be purified by the Logos. When
this has been achieved, Christ's second coming and the resurrection of all men, not in material, but in spiritual bodies,
will follow, and God will be all in all.[11]

Quasten believes that Origen holds the eternal repetition of apos-
tasy and reconciliation, so that the *apokatastasis* (universal restoration) is never a final consummation.[12] Daniélou admits that there
are times when Origen seems to say this, but he finds just as strong
indications that the idea of the good in his system demands a permanent restoration, and he concludes that Origen never succeeded
in resolving the contradiction between the two viewpoints.[13]

5. After Origen

In the preface of the *De principiis,* which survives only in
Rufinus' version of 398 A.D., it is said that "regarding the devil
and his angels, and the opposing influences (*virtutes*), the teaching
of the Church has laid down that these beings exist indeed; but
what they are, or how they exist, it has not explained with sufficient
clearness. This opinion, however, is held by most (*plurimi*), that
the devil was an angel, and that, having become an apostate, he
induced as many of the angels as possible to fall away with himself,
and these up to the present time are called his angels" (6).
This "opinion" of the fall of the devil and his angels as it stands
here appears to have been adjusted to make Origen's views more acceptable to Rufinus' contemporaries.
Origen's doctrine of the preexistence of human souls was not
generally well received (it was finally condemned at the Second
Council of Constantinople in 553), and other aspects of his system
were also opposed or neglected. Although Gregory of Nyssa accepted a version of the *apokatastasis,*[14] he was an exception to the
rule. But the idea that the devil himself and other wicked angels

[11] J. Quasten, *Patrology* II (Utrecht 1953) 87.
[12] *Ibid.* 89-90.
[13] J. Daniélou, *Message évangélique et culture hellénistique aux IIe et IIIe
siècles* (Tournai 1961) 388.
[14] See Daniélou, *Origen* 288-89.

underwent a fall, not because of unauthorized dealings with mankind, as the earlier Fathers believed, but because of a turning away from God in a pre-cosmic situation, as Origen postulated, became the prevailing view.

Therefore, although the more radical portions of Origen's theory were not accepted, many of the Fathers continued to speculate in a similar fashion, but within the restricted framework we have just described. St. Augustine, for instance, in explaining that demons have bodies made of air, says:

> If perchance the angels who transgressed were in that part [where the air is pure and borders on the celestial region above the air] before their transgression, along with their chief, now the devil, but then an archangel (for some of us do not believe that they were celestial or supercelestial angels), it would not be strange if after their sin they were cast down into this dense air (*caligo*). . . . If however those transgressors before they transgressed had celestial bodies it would still not be strange if as a punishment their bodies have been changed to an airy nature, so that they can now suffer from fire, that is, from an element of a higher nature; and that they have not even been allowed to stay in the region of higher and purer air, but must instead remain until judgment day in this dense atmosphere, which is like a dungeon for them according to their kind.[15]

Augustine's thought here is in conformity with the Jewish notion that regarded the various kinds of angels as natural inhabitants of the heavens, that is, of the layers of sky that intervened between God's dwelling place and the earth. It was from one of these heavens, for instance, that the Watchers were thought to have descended to mate with the daughters of men.

Origen eliminated the need to credit the story that the bulk of angels fell through commerce with women and gave birth to demons. St. Augustine, too, had only to identify the demons, who acted as pagan gods and possessing spirits, with the angels whose fall we have just seen him describe. But he kept that aspect of the

[15] Augustine, *De Genesi ad literam* 3, 10 (CSEL 28, 73-74; PL 34, 285).

old story that appears in Jude 6, according to which the fallen angels were imprisoned in "darkness" (*zophos*), which means the darkness of the world beneath the earth, or, as the second epistle of Peter (2, 4) specifies, "Tartarus." The *zophos* of Jude was translated into Latin as *caligo,* which can mean not only "darkness" but also "fog" or "thick air." Augustine was therefore able to identify the prison of the "sinful angels" (2 Pet. 2, 4) "who did not watch over their principality, but abandoned their own dwelling-place" (Jude 6) with the heavenly domain of the Pauline principalities and powers, who are called "the world-rulers of this darkness" (Eph. 6, 12).

The speculations of other theologians went in other directions, and some believed that Satan himself was detained in hell (which was thought to be under the earth), where he would remain until the time of the antichrist; others thought that at least some demons were already in hell, where they served to torture the souls of the damned, or that demons tempted on earth and tormented in hell in shifts. Furthermore, it was generally professed that Lucifer was the most exalted angel in heaven before his fall and transformation into Satan.[16]

Even though Augustine was insistent in his denial that good angels could have fallen through intercourse with women, he could not bring himself to deny that the already fallen angels could and often did carry on in this way, because of the many trustworthy persons who had testified to the phenomenon (*City of God* 15, 23). This judgment of his was used in the Middle Ages and Renaissance to help authorize belief in demonic "nightmares," that is, demons who took on the forms of men (*incubi*) or women (*succubi*) and molested persons sexually. St. Thomas, for instance, cites Augustine's words to this effect in the *Summa theologiae* (1, 51,3 ad 6), and furthermore describes how the "sons of God" of Genesis (6, 1-4), if they are to be understood as demons (that is, fallen angels), could beget giants upon the daughters of men. If a demon were to come as a *succubus* to a larger-than-average man, he could obtain his sperm by intercourse, and then, while safeguarding the vital

---

[16] These opinions are collected in Peter Lombard's *Sentences* (2, 6: PL 192, 662-64), a twelfth-century theological textbook widely used in the medieval universities.

qualities of the sperm and waiting until the stars were in the right conjunction for a felicitous conception, transform himself into an *incubus* and impregnate a woman of ample proportions; the child born of this process would be of a very great size, and could well be designated as a giant (*De potentia* 6, 8 ad 5.7).

We see, then, that the ancient myth of the lustful angels from *Enoch* left its mark on the greatest minds of Christianity even after it had been replaced by a fragment of Origen's philosophical myth. The modified form in which Origen's views were accepted found supporting texts in scripture, and thus a structure was provided that was able to absorb every kind of evil spirit detailed in the mythologies of all the cultures with which the Church came into contact.

6. Cultic Responses to Demonological Theories

(1) *Additional Theories*

We have seen that Origen drew heavily upon Alexandrian religious and philosophical concepts to formulate his world view. But he also shared in the widespread practice of adopting Jewish-Christian notions. Among the demonological concepts he borrows are two that we have not yet discussed, namely, the doctrine of the two angels and the theory of vice-demons.

Origen even specifies his Jewish-Christian sources when he speaks of the two angels: "The book of the *Shepherd* declares . . . that each individual is attended by two angels; that whenever good thoughts arise in our hearts, they are suggested by the good angel; but when of a contrary kind, they are the instigation of the evil angel. The same is declared by Barnabas in his epistle, where he says there are two ways, one of light and one of darkness, over which he asserts that certain angels are placed—the angels of God over the way of light, the angels of Satan over the way of darkness" (*De princ.* 3,2,4). The *Shepherd* of Hermas and the pseudepigraphous *Epistle of Barnabas* are second-century documents that reflect the Qumran doctrine of the Angel of Light and the Angel of Darkness as well as the rabbinic concept of a good and evil inclination within each man. Origen takes up the latter idea specifically elsewhere.[17]

For the strange notion that each kind of vice or sin is under the control of a particular demon, Origen draws upon another Jewish-Christian work, namely, the *Testaments of the Twelve Patriarchs,* which he cites by name in his *Homilies on Joshua* (15, 6). He elaborates the theory's consequences in the *De principiis:*

> A confirmatory evidence of the fact that vices of such enormity proceed from demons may be easily seen in this, that those individuals who are oppressed either by immoderate love, or uncontrollable anger, or excessive sorrow, do not suffer less than those who are bodily vexed by demons. For it is recorded in certain histories, that some have fallen into madness from a state of love, others from a state of anger, not a few from a state of sorrow, and even from one of excessive joy—which results, I think, from this, that those opposing powers, that is, those demons, having gained a lodgment in their minds which has been already laid open to them by intemperance, have taken complete possession of their sensitive nature, especially when no feeling of the glory of virtue has aroused them to resistance. (3,2,2)

(2) *Baptism As Demon-Expelling*

With this kind of connection between sin and demons, it was natural to regard conversion to Christianity and especially baptism as a means of ridding oneself of whatever demons one was infested with. A very clear example of this mentality can be found in the *Clementine Recognitions,* a Syrian pseudepigraphon (purportedly by Clement of Rome) that probably goes back to the early third century in its original form. At one point, Peter is made to say:

> I would have you know for certain, that everyone who has at any time worshipped idols, and has adored those whom the pagans call gods, or has eaten of the things sacrificed to them, is not without an unclean spirit; for he has become a guest of

[17] See Daniélou, *Message évangélique* 401-02.

demons, and has been a partaker with that demon of which he has formed the image in his mind, either through fear or love. And by these means he is not free from an unclean spirit, and therefore needs the purification of baptism, that the unclean spirit may go out of him, which has made its abode in the inmost affections of his soul, and what is worse, gives no indicacation that it lurks within, for fear it should be exposed and expelled. (2, 71 ANF)

This passage is an elaboration of Paul's warning not to become the associates of demons (1 Cor. 10, 20), which, as we saw, undoubtedly referred to dumb idols rather than to living spirits.

(3) *Prebaptismal Exorcism*

It was also a natural development for baptism to be preceded by various rituals designed to purify oneself of demons. The first certain instance of such prebaptismal practices occurs in a gnostic source. Clement of Alexandria preserves the account given by the Valentinian gnostic Theodotus (fl. 160-70 A.D.) of fasts, prayers, impositions (or elevations) of hands, and genuflections before baptism, which have as their purpose the separation of unclean spirits from the candidates (excerpts 83-84).[18]

Clement of Alexandria himself was emphatically opposed to a concept of sin which implied the indwelling of demons. He considered this concept a gnostic aberration, and denied that Barnabas taught it in his epistle. When Barnabas says that before believing in God one's heart was a temple full of idolatry and a house of demons, Clement interprets him as follows:

He says, then, that sinners exercise activities appropriate to demons; but he does not say that the spirits themselves dwell in the soul of the unbeliever. Wherefore he also adds, "See that the temple of the Lord be gloriously built. Learn, having

[18] *Extraits de Théodote* (ed. and tr. F. Sagnard, Sources chrétiennes 23, Paris 1948) 206-09. Earlier descriptions of baptism, such as those of the *Didache* and Justin (*1 Apol.* 61), specify that it is to be preceded by fasts, but there is no indication that the fasting was considered as exorcistic rather than based on the traditional motives of penance and prayer.

received the remission of sins; and having set our hope on the
Name, let us become new, created again from the beginning."
For what he says is not that demons are driven out of us, but
that the sins which like them we commit before believing are
remitted. (*Stromata* 2, 20 ANF)

In spite of Clement's opposition to the philosophy that motivated
pre-baptismal exorcism, the practice spread rapidly during the
course of the third century into the rest of the Christian world, except for parts of Syria, where a strong tradition resisted it and
continues to do so to the present time in the Nestorian and Chaldean
rites. The sin-demon theory soon died away, but the ritual based
upon it has survived it for a millennium and a half.

(4) *The Sin of Adam and Satan's Rule over Mankind*

Contrary to what is commonly supposed, the lack of baptismal
exorcism in East Syrian rites has nothing to do with the alleged
Nestorian rejection of original sin. In fact, as F. J. Dölger has
pointed out, the question of Adam's sin did not enter at all into the
original motivation behind the development of the exorcisms, although later St. Augustine and other opponents of Pelagianism assumed that the opposite was true and attempted to use the practice,
especially when applied to infants, as a proof for an early and
widespread tradition of original sin. The ritual for infant baptism
was simply taken over from the adult ceremony, and infants were
baptized not because they were felt to be sinful in any way but because Jesus had specified that everyone must be baptized (Jn. 3,
5), and also because a parallel was drawn with circumcision, a
ritual that took place on the eighth day after birth.[19]

The fall of man did, of course, eventually find a place in the
ideology of baptism. In the earliest baptistery yet discovered, that
of Dura-Europos in East Syria (second quarter of the third century), there is a picture of Adam and Eve and the serpent by the
tree of knowledge.[20] There is no indication that the serpent is re-

[19] F. J. Dölger, *Der Exorzismus im altchristlichen Taufritual* (Paderborn
1909) 39-43.
[20] See P. V. C. Baur, "Paintings in the Christian Chapel," *The Excavations
at Dura-Europus 5* (ed. M. I. Rostovtzeff, New Haven 1934) 257-58.

garded as Satan, but by that time the identification had become virtually universal. Two centuries later, in the baptismal rituals of East Syria and nearby Cilicia, as described in the homilies of Narsai and Theodore of Mopsuestia, respectively, Satan is envisaged as having received the right to tyrannize mankind because of Adam's sin. Accordingly, the baptismal ceremony is preceded by a trial in which Satan is pictured as coming to demand justice, only to be reminded each time by the candidates' "lawyers" that in unjustly condemning Christ to death he lost control over the whole of humanity.[21]

We see here a variant of the "rights of the devil" theory first hinted at by Irenaeus in the second century and developed by later Fathers, notably Origen and Augustine. According to this fanciful conception Christ exercised a pious fraud upon Satan whereby he nullified the conditions that gave him authority to rule over the world of men. He either induced him to exceed his authority, as in the rituals just described, or he managed to deliver to him a ransom of sufficient worth to effect the release of his captives.

Although the ministers who act as lawyers in Theodore's rite are called exorcists, they do not perform a real exorcism but simply explain the rights of the candidates in the light of the redemption and ask God as judge to agree with them and deny the devil's petition. The candidates are then enrolled and proceed to "renounce Satan, all his angels, all his cult, all his illusion, and all his pomp."

(5) Baptismal Renunciation

The renunciation of Satan is perhaps the best known of the demonological aspects of Christian baptism. Once again we must turn to Clement's excerpts from the writings of Theodotus for the first recorded instance of a renunciation at baptism; in excerpt 77 we read: "For this reason baptism is called death and the end of the old life, since we renounce the evil principalities; and it is called life according to Christ, since he is the sole master of this life."

It is true, however, that the term for renunciation (*apotasses-*

---

[21] *The Liturgical Homilies of Narsai* 22 (tr. R. H. Connolly, Texts and Studies 8, 1, Cambridge 1909) 39; *Les homélies catéchétiques de Théodore de Mopsueste* 12, 18-26 (tr. R. Tonneau with R. Devreesse, Vatican City 1949).

thai) was used earlier in more general, though still demonic, contexts: Hermas says that "it is good to follow the angel of justice and to renounce the angel of evil," and Justin describes pagan converts as renouncing idols and adhering to God through Christ.[22] Daniélou suggests that the actual formula of renunciation may come from the ritual of the Essenes, because of their doctrine of the two ways, or two spirits, of good and evil.[23] But in the surviving descriptions of the ceremony of initiation at Qumran the parallel is not very close. The candidates first agree to be converted to the law of Moses, and then undertake "to be separated from all perverse men who walk in the way of wickedness" (1 QS 5,8-11). The service does, however, also involve a confession of the sins that were committed under Belial (1, 22-26).[24]

In more orthodox circles, the earliest formulas for the pre-baptismal renunciation of Satan come from the beginning of the third century—in Africa, as reported by Tertullian, and Rome, in the *Apostolic Tradition* of Hippolytus. Their principal purpose is the forswearing of the practices of idolatry, which, as we have seen, was considered to be the worship of the evil spirits.

(6) *Material Elements and Gestures*

Still another feature of the baptismal service with a demonological basis is the exorcism of the water used in baptism. Once again it is in the gnostic excerpts from Theodotus that this ceremony first appears. The result of the exorcism is said to be the "separation of the inferior element" and the sanctification of the water. The bread and oil used in the ritual are also sanctified by the invocation of the name of God (exc. 82).

Dölger believes that ideas about demons living in the water is a phenomenon common to the folklore of pagans, Jews, and Christians alike, and we see the notion taken seriously by Tertullian in his treatise on baptism (c. 5).[25] Eventually prayers were introduced into the rites which were designed both to drive away the evil spirits that might be in or near the water and to give to the

---

[22] Hermas, *Shepherd* 36, 9 GCS (=Mandate 6, 2, 9); Justin, *1 Apol.* 49. Christ uses the same word when demanding that one leave behind all possessions (Lk 14, 33).
[23] Daniélou, *Theol. of Jewish Christianity* 321-22.
[24] In Dupont-Summer, *Essene Writings* 74. 83.
[25] Dölger, *Exorzismus* 161. 163. Some authors, such as A. Benoit, *Le*

water the virtue of repelling any future demonic attack. Consecrated water of this sort gradually came to be used in numerous contexts apart from baptism. Similar prayers were inserted for the exorcism and consecration of the salt and oil used at baptism, and these exorcized substances in time became ingredients of baptismal as well as of non-baptismal holy water.[26]

The gnostic sect to which Theodotus belonged seems to provide the earliest example of yet another rite of initiation that became generally used in Christendom, that of marking catechumens with the sign of the cross (exc. 42).[27] There is no indication whether the ceremony already had an apotropaic (that is, demon-repelling) significance, but by the beginning of the third century this function of the sign of the cross was very much in evidence. In the *Apostolic Tradition* of Hippolytus it is recommended that one sign oneself when tempted, thereby forcing the devil away, as the destroying angel was turned away from the Israelites in Egypt who sprinkled blood on their doors.

In time the sign of the cross became an element in the blessing of water. An early instance is reported in the *Panarion* of Epiphanius of Cyprus (fourth century), who tells of the cure of a maniac in which signed water was used. The water was sprinkled over the victim and the demon ordered to depart from him in the name of Jesus crucified.[28]

Other means for warding off demons were developed through the centuries, so much so that at the present time, according to the study of Cipriano Vagaggini, the demonic motif figures not only in all seven sacraments of the Catholic computation, but in about fifty sacramentals as well.[29]

---

baptême chrétienne au sec*u*nd siècle (Paris 1953) 67-69, have sought to find similar notions in earlier Christian writers, such as Ignatius of Antioch, but their arguments are not convincing.

[26] See Elmar Bartsch, *Die Sachbeschwörungen der römischen Liturgie* (Münster 1967).

[27] Cf. F. J. Dölger's posthumous work, "Beiträge zur Geschichte des Kreuzzeichens," *Jahrbuch für Antike und Christentum* 4 (1961) 11.

[28] Epiphanius, *Panarion* heresy 30, 10 (GCS 25, 345).

[29] C. Vagaggini, *Theological Dimensions of the Liturgy* (tr. L. J. Doyle, Collegeville 1959) c. 13: "The Two Cities: the Struggle Against Satan in the Liturgy" 200-42 (esp. 228), an abridgment of *Il senso teologico della liturgia* (Rome 1957) 279-349.

(7) *Protestant Reforms*

It is still in the ceremonies connected with baptism that we can find the greatest amount of demonological material, especially in Catholic and Orthodox rituals. At the time of the Reformation, some of the exorcisms were taken over by Luther and his followers (though not the exorcisms of water, salt, and oil), but they were soon discarded. The renunciation of Satan has proved more durable, and remains in the Anglican Church and in most Lutheran confessions. The Church of Sweden is an exception, however, since the existence of the devil came into question on philosophical and theological grounds in Sweden in the last century. But in America the Swedish Lutheran Church recovered the ceremony of renunciation when it merged with other branches to form the Lutheran Church in America. Calvinist denominations, such as the Presbyterians and the Congregationalists (the latter are now in the United Church of Christ), did not take over the renunciation at all. The chief reason no doubt was that the ceremony was not scriptural. This neglect of the form of renunciation had nothing to do with a weakening of belief in the devil among Calvinists, for, as we shall see in the next chapter, Satan flourished in men's minds at the time of the Reformation to a greater degree than ever before or since.[30]

[30] The anti-demonic ceremonies centering around the rite of baptism are treated more fully in H. A. Kelly, *The Demonology of Christian Initiation* (forthcoming).

III
DEMONIC WITCHCRAFT

In the context of Christian demonology, witchcraft means any human activity attributed to the help of evil spirits. From the theological point of view, there is no difference between witchcraft, sorcery, and magic. Historically the concept of demonic witchcraft assumed its greatest importance in Western Europe from the fifteenth to the seventeenth century, during the large-scale witch persecutions.

In tracing the development of the theory behind the witch-hunts, we can discern a familiar pattern in the interaction between accepted beliefs and new circumstances, which resulted in a new synthesis. Fresh superstitions were accepted as factual and interpreted in terms of the diabolical; that is, they were incorporated into the system of demonology whose formulations we have studied in their successive transformations from earliest Christian times.

1. The Biblical and Patristic Setting

When discussing episodes or passages in the bible relating to witchcraft, we must remember that everything was interpreted by Christians in the light of non-biblical stories or theories of fallen angels and evil demons.

According to the *Book of Enoch,* the angelic Watchers "took unto themselves wives, and each chose for himself one, and they began to go in unto them and to defile themselves with them, and they taught them charms and enchantments, and the cutting of roots, and made them acquainted with plants" (7, 1). Here already in the second century before Christ we see foreshadowed many of the characteristics that will be found in "Christian witchcraft."

One of the most significant steps in the development of the

Christian notion of witchcraft was the identification of the fallen angels with the pagan gods. We recall Justin saying that these angels and their demon offspring enslaved the human race "partly by magical writings, and partly by fears and the punishments they occasioned, and partly by teaching them to offer sacrifices and incense and libations, of which things they stood in need after they were enslaved by lustful passions" (2 Apol. 5).

In refuting Trypho's opinion that it was blasphemous to suggest that angels sinned and revolted against God, Justin goes to the Old Testament and cites, among other things, the episode of the magicians of Pharaoh who attempted to match the miracles worked by God through Moses (Dial. 79); later he says the encounter of Saul with the so-called Witch of Endor and the dead Samuel (1 Sam. 28) shows that "all the souls of similar righteous men and prophets fell under the dominion of such powers," that is, evil angels (Dial. 105).

Other Fathers of the Church shared Justin's view that the Witch of Endor had demonic connections, and a prominent interpretation was that it was actually a demon and not the shade of Samuel that spoke to Saul.[1] The Hebrew word for necromancer in this episode is translated as "ventriloquist" in the Septuagint, and in the Latin Vulgate as "a woman having a python." In Leviticus such persons are condemned to death; the Latin here speaks of those "in whom there is a pythonic or divining spirit" (20, 27).

In the Acts of the Apostles, Paul and his companions encountered a girl "having a python spirit" that continually pointed them out as servants of God who were preaching the way of salvation. After many days of this Paul finally reached the limit of his patience and ordered the spirit to go out of the girl in the name of Jesus Christ (Acts 16, 16-18). Elsewhere Paul condemned "witchcraft" in the sense of the making use of potions or charms (pharmakeia: Gal. 5, 20), and when he confronted the Jewish magician and false prophet Barjesus, or Elymas, Paul called him a "child of the devil" (Acts 13, 6-11). We have seen that this epithet was one that was applied to all sinners, but it came to be reserved especially for the preachers of heresy or false doctrines.

[1] See the texts of the Greek Fathers gathered under the entry daimon (G. 1) in G. W. H. Lampe, A Patristic Greek Lexicon 2 (Oxford 1962) 330-31.

Simon Magus is another magician who appears in Acts. We are told nothing of the nature of his magic, except that the people of Samaria found it very impressive, but not as impressive as Simon himself found the signs performed by the heralds of Christianity. We hear no more of him except that after his conversion to Christianity he attempted to purchase the power of imparting the Holy Spirit by the imposition of hands, and that when Peter rebuked him for it he asked for pardon (Acts 8, 9-24).

Simon was honored as a divinity in a Samaritan sect, which is one of the earliest known forms of the gnostic religion. It is not clear how much of a role Simon himself played in the development of Simonism (as we may call it), but later Christian writers consider him to be the father of all heresies, and to have been supported in all his activities by Satan and his fellow demons. This tradition begins with Justin, who writes:

> There was a Samaritan, Simon, a native of the village called Gitto, who in the reign of Claudius Caesar, and in your royal city of Rome, did mighty acts of magic, by virtue of the art of the demons operating in him. He was considered a god, and as a god was honored by you with a statue, which was erected on the river Tiber between the two bridges, and bore this inscription, in the language of Rome, *Simoni deo sancto,* "To Simon the holy God." (*1 Apol.* 26)

That Simon was ever in Rome is doubtful, since Justin seems to have based the account of his sojourn there on a mistaken reading of an inscription to an old Sabine deity, Semo Sancus. But Simon's alleged activities in Rome underwent fanciful developments in later writings, beginning with the apocryphal *Acts of Peter,* written towards the end of the second century, most probably in Asia Minor. We read here of a running battle between Simon and Peter, which culminates in a confrontation at Rome. Simon attempts to prove that he is from God by flying up to heaven; he does indeed succeed in flying, but at Peter's prayer he falls to the earth, discredited and crippled for life.[2]

The mechanism of Simon's flight was, of course, to be ex-

[2] *Acts of Peter* 5; 32 (James, *Apocryphal New Testament* 307; 331-32).

plained by the demons who assisted him. This is made explicit in later versions of the story, such as the *Acts of the Holy Apostles Peter and Paul,* where we read:

> Peter, looking steadfastly against Simon, said: "I adjure you, ye angels of Satan, who are carrying him into the air to deceive the hearts of the unbelievers, by the God that created all things, and by Jesus Christ, whom on the third day he raised from the dead, no longer from this hour to keep him up, but to let him go." And immediately, being let go, he fell into a place called Sacra Via, that is, Holy Way, and was divided into four parts, having perished by an evil fate. (ANF)

We find in these texts many of the ingredients that will make up the concoction of medieval witchcraft—the worship paid to demons by the practitioners of magic, association with "familiar spirits," the use of demons to perform prodigies like flying through the air and the revealing of occult knowledge, and the sexual commerce of fallen spirits with human beings.

A prototype of the diabolical pact which all witches were later believed to make, either explicitly or implicitly, may be found in Satan's offer of all the kingdoms of the world to Jesus if only he would fall down and worship him (Mt. 4, 8-9). This temptation, which Jesus successfully resisted, could be regarded as exactly the same kind of allurement to which Doctor Faustus succumbed.

St. Augustine contributed to the development of the concept of the witch-pact when he warned against indulging in divination even when it could produce valid results:

> For though the image of the dead Samuel foretold the truth to King Saul, that does not make such sacrilegious observances as those by which his image was presented the less detestable; and though the ventriloquist woman in the Acts of the Apostles bore true testimony to the apostles of the Lord, the apostle Paul did not spare the evil spirit on that account, but rebuked and cast it out, and so made that woman clean. All arts of this sort, therefore, are either nullities, or are part of a guilty superstition, springing out of a baleful fellowship between men

and demons, and are to be utterly repudiated and avoided by the Christian as the covenants (*pacta*) of a false and treacherous friendship.[3]

This passage from Augustine was incorporated by Gratian in the twelfth century into his *Decretum*,[4] the great medieval textbook of canon law.

Another source that contributed to the medieval portrait of the witch was the descriptions of sorceresses in Horace and other authors of classical antiquity. Julio Caro Beroja says:

There is documentary evidence of the existence over a period of *centuries* of the belief that certain women (not necessarily old ones) could change themselves and others at will into animals in classical times; that they could fly through the air by night and enter the most secret and hidden places by leaving their body behind; that they could make spells and potions to further their own love affairs or to inspire hatred for others; that they could bring about storms, illness both in men and animals, and strike fear into their enemies or play terrifying jokes on them. To carry out their evil designs these women met together after dark. The moon, night, Hecate, and Diana were the deities who presided over them, helping them to make philters and potions. They called on these goddesses for aid in their poetic conjurations, or threatened and constrained them in their spells when they wanted to achieve particularly difficult results.[5]

When Christians encountered tales of this sort their first reaction was often to doubt their factualness, but if the testimony or evidence for the alleged phenomena were of sufficient weight, they would account for them in demonological terms. We find both re-

---

[3] Augustine, *De doctrina christiana* 2, 88-89 = 2, 23 (CSEL 80, ed. W. M. Green, Wien 1963) 59; tr. adap. NPNF.

[4] Gratian, *Decretum* 2, 26, 2, 6 (*Illud quod est*), *Corpus iuris canonici* (ed. E. Friedberg, Leipzig 1879 repr. Graz 1959) I 1021-22.

[5] J. Caro Beroja, *The World of the Witches* (Chicago 1964) 39-40 (an often inadequate translation by O. N. V. Glendinning of *Las brujas y su mundo*, Madrid 1961).

actions in St. Augustine when he is discussing stories of zoanthropy, that is, of transformations of men into animals. He mentions not only literary descriptions, such as that by Apuleius in the *Golden Ass,* but also the reports he himself heard while he was in Italy "about a certain region there, where landladies of inns, imbued with these wicked arts, were said to be in the habit of giving such travelers as they chose, or could manage, something in a piece of cheese by which they were changed on the spot into beasts of burden, and carried whatever was necessary, and were restored to their own form when the work was done." He concludes:

These things are either false, or so extraordinary as to be with good reason disbelieved. But it is to be most firmly believed that almighty God can do whatever he pleases, whether in punishing or favoring, and that demons can accomplish nothing by their natural power (for their created being is itself angelic, although made malign by their own fault), except what he may permit, whose judgments are often hidden, but never unrighteous. And indeed the demons, if they really do such things as these on which this discussion turns, do not create real substances, but only change the appearance of things created by the true God so as to make them seem to be what they are not. I cannot therefore believe that even the body, much less the mind, can really be changed into bestial forms and lineaments by any reason, art, or power of the demons; but the phantasm of a man which even in thought or dreams goes through innumerable changes, may, when the man's senses are laid asleep or overpowered, be presented to the senses of others in a corporeal form, in some indescribable way unknown to me, so that men's bodies themselves may lie somewhere, alive, indeed, yet with their senses locked up much more heavily and firmly than by sleep, while that phantasm, as it were embodied in the shape of some animal, may appear to the senses of others, and may even seem to the man himself to be changed, just as he may seem to himself in sleep to be so changed, and to bear burdens; and these burdens, if they are real substances, are borne by the demons, that men may be deceived by beholding at the same time the real substance of the burdens and the simulated bodies of the beasts of burden. (*City of God* 18, 18 NPNF)

What seems to be an example of total incredulity in the feats of witches can be found in Ireland in the so-called "Synod of St. Patrick," which may go back almost to the time of St. Augustine. Canon 16 of this set of regulations threatens punishment for belief in witchcraft, rather than for its practice.[6] But most probably the Irish ecclesiastical authorities would not have denied the possibility of all diabolically assisted prodigies. The regulation does, however, give evidence of a critical spirit, which seems to have been more common among missionaries than among a native clergy that had inherited the superstitions of its environment.

Many of the early civil laws show a similar moderation in describing the effects of the forbidden practices of magic. For instance, during the reign of Constantine the following law was issued, and later incorporated into the *Theodosian Code:*

The science of those men who are equipped with magic arts and who are revealed to have worked against the safety of men or to have turned virtuous minds to lust shall be punished and deservedly avenged by the most severe laws. (TC 9,16,3, A.D. 317-19) [7]

However, the interpretation of this law that was added to the *Code* sometime between its promulgation in 438 and the production of the *Breviarium of Alaric* in 506 injects a very definite supernatural element into the magic: "Magicians, enchanters, conjurers of storms, or those persons who through invocation of demons throw into confusion the minds of men shall be punished with every kind of penalty."

Another instance of this kind of development can be seen in the

[6] See L. Bieler, "Patrick's Synod: a Revision," *Mélanges offerts à Mlle. Christine Mohrmann* (Utrecht 1963) 96-102, who argues for a mid-fifth-century date.
[7] Tr. Clyde Pharr, *The Theodosian Code and Novels and the Sirmondian Constitutions* (Princeton 1952) 237. Cf. A. A. Barb, "The Survival of Magic Arts" in *The Conflict Between Paganism and Christianity in the Fourth Century* (ed. Arnaldo Momigliano, Oxford 1963) 100-25.

law passed under the Emperors Valentinian and Valens in the year 364, which reads:

> Hereafter no person shall attempt during the nighttime to engage in wicked prayers or magic preparations or funereal sacrifices. If he should be detected and convicted of such practices, We decree by Our everlasting authority that he shall be stricken with a suitable punishment. (TC 9,16,7)

The interpretation, however, reads: "If any person should celebrate nocturnal sacrifices to the demons or should invoke the demons by incantations, he shall suffer capital punishment."

2. Medieval Developments

The fragmented Frankish empire of the ninth century, which gave rise to the false decretals of Pseudo-Isidore, was the home also of an important forgery that touched upon the subject of witchcraft. Just as the earliest collections of ecclesiastical canons were promulgated in a pseudepigraphous form that attributed them to the apostles or to Christ himself, these later documents were ascribed to the early councils and popes. The witchcraft canon, which was incorporated into Gratian's *Decretum* and known as *Episcopi eorumque* from its opening words, first appears in the capitularies of Charles the Bald for the year 872,[8] and is ascribed to the fourth-century Council of Ancyra (Ankara). The canon reads as follows:

> Bishops and their ministers are to labor with all their might thoroughly to eradicate from their parishioners the pernicious practice of divination and magic, which was invented by the devil; and if they find any man or woman who indulges in this kind of crime, they are to cast him out from among their parishioners as foully disgraced. For the apostle says, "Shun the heretical man after the first and second correction, knowing that such a one is subverted." They are subverted and

[8] Caro, *World* 61.

held captive by the devil who leave their creator and seek the aid of the devil, and therefore the holy Church should be cleansed of such a plague.

Nor is it to be overlooked that certain depraved women who have turned back after Satan and been seduced by the illusions and fantasies of demons believe and profess that they ride on various beasts during the night hours along with Diana, the goddess of the pagans, [later addition: or with Herodias] and a countless multitude of women, and pass across many areas of the earth in the dead of the unwholesome night; and that they obey her commands as those of a mistress, and on certain nights are summoned to her service. But would that it were only these who have perished in their perfidy, and that they had not dragged many others with them to the perdition of infidelity. For a countless multitude have been deceived by this false opinion and believe these things to be true, and in so believing turn away from the true faith and become entangled in the error of the pagans, in thinking that there is some divinity or deity other than the one God. For this reason priests should preach with all diligence to the people of God in the churches assigned to them, so that they may know that these things are completely false, and that such fantasies are called up in the minds of the faithful not by the divine but by the evil spirit.

That is to say, when Satan himself, who transforms himself into an angel of light, has taken hold of the mind of each of these women and subdued her to himself by her infidelity, he then transforms himself into the appearance and likeness of various persons and deludes the mind he holds captive during times of sleep, alternating happy visions with sad, and known persons with unknown, leading them through every kind of crooked path; and though the unfaithful woman experiences all this only in the spirit she believes that it happens not in the mind but in the flesh. For who is there that is not drawn out of himself in sleep and in nightly visions and does not see many things while asleep that he has never seen awake? But who would be so stupid and dull-witted as to think that all these things that happen in the spirit alone also take place in the flesh? Just so the prophet Ezekiel saw and heard visions of the Lord in the spirit, not in the flesh, as he himself declares: "All at once," he says, "I was in the spirit." And Paul did not dare to say that he was taken up in the flesh. Therefore everyone should be publicly informed that whoever believes these and similar things loses his faith, and whoever does not have true faith [in God] belongs not to him but to the one in whom he believes, that is, the devil. For it is written of our Lord, "All things were made through him." Whoever, therefore, believes it possible for any creature to be changed for better or worse or to be transformed into another appearance or likeness except by the Creator himself who made all things and through whom all things were made, is without doubt an infidel, and worse than a pagan.[9]

The passage from the *City of God* on the question of zoanthropy quoted above would provide a theologically acceptable explanation for the activity that the forged canon branded as an illusion, in case it should turn out to have some basis in fact; that is, if the women really did fly through the air and have nocturnal meetings, it was the devil who transported them.

Just what, if anything, corresponded in reality to the practices ascribed to witches in accusations and confessions during the era of persecution is a question that has been much debated in the twentieth century. There are not many authors who share the beliefs of the witch-hunters in the actuality and diabolical nature of the alleged occurrences. A notable exception is Montague Summers, whose many books on demonology he authored under the guise of a Catholic priest, but whose ordination to the priesthood, if it ever took place, was not recognized as licit by Church authorities.[10]

Another, much more popular, theory is that propounded by Margaret Murray in *The Witch-cult in Western Europe* (1921), *The God of the Witches* (1933), and *The Divine King in England* (1954), according to which a highly organized prehistoric religion was the object of ecclesiastical and civil persecutions. Even though her more extravagant theses of later years have not won wide-

[9] Gratian, *Decretum* 2, 26, 5, 12 (*Episcopi eorumque*) Friedberg I 1030-31.
[10] See Joseph Jerome, *Montague Summers* (London 1965) xiii; 11-23.

spread approval, there is a surprising number of scholars (not usually historians) who believe that her original analysis is fundamentally valid. Her authority was such that she was asked to write the entry on witchcraft for the fourteenth edition of the *Encyclopaedia Britannica,* and her essay has been retained in all subsequent issues up to the present day.

However, even in her early writings her method does not inspire confidence in the soundness of her judgments, and most historians of witchcraft have dismissed her conclusions as unproved.[11] We may illustrate the weakness of her approach by quoting from the above-mentioned encyclopedia article. She begins her discussion by citing Coke's definition of a witch as "a person who hath conference with the Devil to consult with him or to do some act." She continues:

> The word "devil" (*q.v.*) is a diminutive from the root "div," from which we also get the word "divine." It merely means "little god." It is a well-known fact that when a new religion is established in any country, the god or gods of the old religion become the devil of the new.[12]

If Miss Murray had followed the suggestion of the editors and looked up the *Britannica* article on "Devil," she might have discovered the true derivation of the word. It comes, as we have seen, from the Greek translation of the Hebrew *satan;* the *de* element corresponds to the prepositional prefix *dia* ("through") and the *vil* element to *ballein* ("to throw"). Needless to say, "divine" has a totally different etymology.

Furthermore, it is not true that a divinity in one religion invariably becomes a devil in the religion that replaces it, as Miss Murray suggests, whether one defines devil in her bizarre sense of subordinate deity, or in the more usual sense of evil spirit. There are many ways of resolving such a religious conflict. For instance, when the Israelites confronted the Canaanite nature religion, they

[11] For a recent critique of her work, see Geoffrey Parrinder, *Witchcraft: European and African* (London 1963) 103-12; she is moderately defended by Sir Steven Runciman in the Foreword to the Oxford reprint of her *Witch cult* (1962, 1963, 1967).
[12] M. Murray, "Witchcraft," *Encyclopaedia Britannica* (ed. 14, London 1929) 23, 686.

54

used, from time to time, three different methods—namely, syncretism (that is, Yahweh was identified with one of the Canaanite gods), suppression, and subordination.[13] We touched upon the last-named process at some length in the first chapter when discussing the origin and function of the angels. These three methods were also used upon occasion in Christian times. Pagan gods were sometimes identified with saints, or were dismissed as superstitious figments, or were transformed into new saints. But the most common approach was, as we saw, to identify them with fallen angels, who, though they wrongfully claimed divine honors, were in no sense regarded as gods, not even as "little gods."

Just as the pagan deities that were recognized as such were assimilated to the evil spirits by the early Christian theologians, whatever relics of pagan beliefs survived among the people (and there undoubtedly were some) were, it may be safely assumed, ordinarily interpreted by later theologians as diabolical. As always, of course, the current superstitions were liable to undergo a transformation as they were recorded and had traditional concepts brought to bear upon them. Caro suggests, for example, that the Frankish author of the pseudo-Ancyran canon *Episcopi eorumque* may have been drawing more upon Horace's description of witches than upon contemporary reports.

The explanation of witchcraft that has received the most respectful attention in modern times is that the conspiratorial aspects that emerged in the witch trials and the writings of demonologists, such as the reports of sabbaths, or orgiastic meetings with the devil, were almost entirely the invention of authorities who forced these concepts upon their victims by means of torture and leading questions. Local superstitions and the scattered remains of pagan customs no doubt played a role in the formation of these ideas, as did practices (real or supposed) of religious sects like that of the Cathari or Albigensians, a Manichean group whose existence is far better authenticated than Miss Murray's ancient cult of the horned god.

But while there is little evidence for the continued existence of a clearly defined prehistoric witch sect in the Middle Ages, it is possible that there emerged, at least in some areas, what could be

[13] Cf. G. B. Caird, *Principalities and Powers* (Oxford 1956) 1.

called a new cult of witchcraft that resulted from a combination of folk superstition and heretical practices. The "new sect" of heretical witchcraft appeared first in the mountain districts that had been the stronghold of the recently suppressed Cathari and Vaudois, that is, the French Pyrenees and Alps. Arne Runeberg offers a hypothetical explanation for this apparent coincidence:

> When the Catharists retired to . . . the inaccessible valleys of southern France and of the Alps, they came into contact with a population among which superstitious beliefs and practices had always flourished. Now, in the same period the inquisitors had begun to extend their activity to include popular sorcerers and magicians, who were often condemned and burned together with the heretics. It seems rather natural then that persecuted Manicheans and magicians should have joined in their hopeless struggle against the persecutors. In this way there might develop a new sort of anti-Catholic or even anti-Christian secret society, based in part on the traditions of the Catharist secret societies . . . in part on popular traditions . . . of pagan origin.[14]

Caro too points out that, when the concept of the witches' sabbath first appears, in inquisitorial trials in the Carcassonne and Toulouse regions early in the fourteenth century, the nature of the accusations cannot be explained by the use of torture.[15] They could however, be based on dreams or hallucinations.

Granted that meetings took place in that part of France that corresponded to the descriptions of the sabbath, it would not follow that the activity itself or the sect responsible for it spread to all the regions in which it came to be suspected. Once the concept became viable in the minds of the authorities, torture and other forms of judicial pressure would be sufficient to explain its pres-

---

[14] A. Runeberg, *Witches, Demons, and Fertility Magic; Analysis of Their Significance and Mutual Relations in West-European Folk Religion* (Societas scientiarum fennica, Commentationes humanarum litterarum 14, 4, Helsingfors 1947) 22-24.

[15] Caro, *World* 84-87. H. T. Trevor-Roper in his essay on the witch-craze in *Religion, the Reformation, and Social Change* (London 1967) continues to believe that the new accusations, though inspired by the cultural and mental aberrations of the mountaineers, were mostly due to the imagination of the Dominican inquisitors.

ence in the trial records. In a letter of Pope John XXII, written from Avignon on July 28, 1319, we can see a very early instance of the application in other areas of the methods used at Toulouse. He is addressing a cleric of the diocese of Poitiers and recounts an episode that occurred when he was an ecclesiastical judge:

> When a certain woman who was publicly infamous for crimes of witchcraft and heretical depravity was brought before you and accused of these crimes and was unwilling to confess anything concerning the said crimes, you, on the advice of certain upright men who said they had seen heretics in the territories of Toulouse examined while pain was inflicted, caused the soles of the said woman's feet to be placed near burning coals, who, when she felt the heat and burning of the same, confessed to very many erroneous and horrendous things against the Catholic faith and revealed many of her associates and accomplices in the said errors, who were afterwards condemned according to their just deserts; all of which things thus discovered, as is commonly believed, would never have been revealed if the aforesaid woman had not revealed them because of these same tortures.[16]

Whatever the basis in reality for the actions attributed to the witches, as they were systematized by the theologians, they had enough similarity to inherited concepts, many of which we have seen, to be incorporated into the theories of traditional Christian demonology without further ado.

An example of this process has been recently brought to light by Carlo Ginzburg, who recounts the history of the *benandanti*

---

[16] J. M. Vidal, *Bullaire de l'inquisition française au XIVᵉ siècle et jusqu'à la fin du grand schisme* (Paris 1913) 51-52. The pope goes on to say that the woman persevered in admitting to the things she had confessed; she was kept in the prison of the bishop of Poitiers while her sentence was being deliberated upon, and while there she died, long after making the aforesaid confession. However, the judge feared that she died sooner than she might have if she had not been tortured, and that he had thereby incurred an irregularity, in spite of the fact that he had consented to it for the zealous defense of the Catholic faith. The pope accordingly granted him whatever dispensation was necessary.

or "good walkers" of Friuli. These were men whose souls supposedly left their bodies during sleep and fought with evil male witches for the protection of their crops, and who were regarded as the practitioners of benevolent magic. Ginzburg suggests that their observances were those of a fertility cult at one time found throughout central Europe, but surviving only in marginal regions in the late sixteenth century, when the Friuli group was brought to the attention of the Church.[17] A reviewer points out the significance of Ginzburg's investigations:

The Holy Inquisition (not unhampered both by its representatives' ignorance of the Friulan dialect and the suspicions of the Venetian Republic) did not quite know what to make of the "good walkers." It therefore attempted to assimilate them to the well-classified and heretical practice of witchcraft, and to press its victims to admit their participation in the diabolist sabbaths. What is more, it succeeded. A series of inquisitions and trials stretching from the 1570's to the 1640's . . . show the "good walkers" gradually assimilating themselves to witches (though attempting to maintain their benevolent functions) under the pressure of the now alerted Church. . . .

The story is local, but its relevance to the general study of the "witch-cult" is obvious. For here we have not Margaret Murray's subterranean old religion hostile to Christianity but ritual practices which had long established a symbiosis with the dominant religion—the *benandanti* originally regarded themselves as champions of Christ against the devil —but which are forced into opposition (one of the accused thought their practices were similar to those of the "Turks, Jews, and Heretics") by Church policy.[18]

[17] C. Ginzburg, *I benandanti; ricerche sulla stregoneria e sui culti agrari tra Cinquecento e Seicento* (Turin 1966) xv.
[18] *Times Literary Supplement* 65 (6 Oct. 1966) 923.

58

3. The Inquisition

It was natural for suspected witches to be punished by the normal legal sanctions for whatever crimes they were thought to have
committed, such as causing personal injury or damaging property,
in the same way that one would be punished for committing these
misdeeds in a non-magical way. This was the traditional procedure,
and when Alexander IV in 1254 gave instructions to the newly
constituted Inquisition, he made it clear that witchcraft did not
fall within its province, but was to be taken care of by the ordinary authorities as in the past. His words, which were incorporated into canon law, are:

> Since the interests of the faith, which enjoy the highest pre-
> rogatives, should not be impeded by other occupations, those
> appointed by the apostolic see as inquisitors against the
> plague of heresy should not concern themselves with divina-
> tion or sortilege, unless it manifestly savors of heresy, nor
> punish those who practice it, but leave their punishment to
> their own judges.[19]

However, it was quite easy to detect heretical views in superstitious beliefs, as we saw in the *Episcopi* canon, where the people
were blamed for believing that there were other divinities than
the one God, and that they had the power of creation. Eventually
the infidelity or defective faith that was detected in all witches
came to be considered as the equivalent of heresy.

The Inquisition has often received the greater share of the blame
for originating and carrying out the persecution of witches, and
this view is still widely held. Rossell Hope Robbins, for instance,
states: "Were it not for the Inquisition, the Catholic tribunal
charged with exposing and punishing religious unorthodoxy, not one

[19] *Liber sextus decretalium* 5, 2, 8 (*Accusatus*) 4 (Friedberg II 1072).

person would have died for witchcraft." [20] A more balanced judgment seems called for, however. As Lynn Thorndike points out,

It is possible to overemphasize the somewhat tenuous connection between magic and heresy. The witch was probably to some extent a scapegoat for the ills which then oppressed society. When we reflect that by the fifteenth century medieval culture was declining; that economic prosperity, political freedom and self-government, chivalry, and public charity were waning; that the fourteenth century had been marked by the terrible Black Death which demoralized society and never ceased its visitations thenceforth during the entire time of the witchcraft delusion, and by the perhaps worse pest of mercenary soldiers who, aided by artillery and firearms, made all wars from the Hundred Years' to the Thirty Years' so cruel, devastating, and financially exhausting—when we consider this, we may incline to regard the witchcraft delusion as in congenial company, and to view it as a sociological rather than theological or intellectual phenomenon, produced largely by popular fear and superstition, and by an undiscriminating wave of "law-enforcement" which swept over the secular more than the ecclesiastical courts, and raged in lands where the Inquisition had hardly functioned.

. . . Among the many records of early trials by the Inquisition which have been preserved there are practically none for magic until Pope John XXII (1316-34), alarmed by attempts against his life made through sorcery and wax images by Hugh Gérard, Bishop of Cahors, the Visconti, and others, started the persecution of magicians in southern France which was continued by Benedict XII. But before this Philip the Fair had preferred charges of abominable magic against the Templars; Guichard, Bishop of Troyes, had been imprisoned in the Louvre for years on like grounds; and sorcery had been among the accusations trumped up against Hubert de Burgh in England under Henry III; so that there is no reason for giving the papacy precedence in magic-baiting.

[20] R. H. Robbins, *The Encyclopedia of Witchcraft and Demonology* (New York 1959) 266, under "Inquisition."

During the years from 1230 to 1430 the number of trials for magic before secular judges was large and ever growing. . . . We may agree, however, . . . that in so far as the witchcraft delusion was led up to by previous writings, it received countenance from works of theologians, canonists, and inquisitors rather than from medieval writers on nature and medicine, who were far more inclined to account for the supposed magical activities of demons by natural causes or human imagination.[21]

The anti-feminism of the age also played an important role in the witch persecution and turned it principally against female suspects.[22] The notorious *Malleus maleficarum* or "Hammer of She-witches" by the two Dominican friars Jakob Sprenger and Heinrich Institoris has been characterized as one of the most anti-feminist books ever written. Sprenger and Institoris had been confirmed in their role as inquisitors by a bull of Innocent VIII, *Summis desiderantes affectibus,* issued in 1484, which complained of various evil practices of witches, such as, for example, sexual intercourse with demons, the causing of injury and disease, and the interfering with conception and birth. In the *Malleus,* which was published shortly afterwards, the two inquisitors took up all these points in great detail and provided a handbook for succeeding generations of persecutors.

In analyzing the concern of the *Malleus* for sexual offenses, W. H. Trethowan believes that the authors were most gravely concerned about "injuries towards men," and finds in their work "much that a psychoanalyst would at once interpret as castration anxiety." He considers it representative of the sadistic tendencies that naturally arose from the suppressed sexual desires of the celibate clergy.[23] In so saying, however, he neglects to take into consideration the important secular manifestations of misog-

21 L. Thorndike, "Magic, Witchcraft, Astrology, and Alchemy," in *The Close of the Middle Ages* (Cambridge Medieval History 8, New York 1936) 686-87; cf. his *History of Magic and Experimental Science* (8 vols., New York 1923-58).
22 See Émile Brouette, "The Sixteenth Century and Witchcraft," in *Satan* (New York 1952) 310-15.
23 W. H. Trethowan, "The Demonopathology of Impotence," *British Journal of Psychiatry* 109 (1963) 341-47.

yny, as well as the role of the secular jurists in the persecution of witches.

Trethowan also overlooks the fact that impotence caused by witchcraft was a concern of ecclesiastical lawyers for centuries before they turned their attention to extirpating a heretical sect of witches. Their interest centered around the effect of impotence on the validity of marriage. Hincmar, the ninth-century arch-bishop of Rheims, originated the discussion when he said that couples might separate when intercourse had been prevented by sorcery.[24] In the thirteenth century a whole section of canon law took up problems "Concerning frigid and bewitched persons and the inability to have intercourse." [25] It was a sign that witchcraft was at work if a man was impotent only towards his wife and not towards other women. In his commentary on the *Sentences* of Peter Lombard, St. Thomas can explain this phenomenon—which today we call selective impotence—only on the supposition that a demon at the direction of a witch withholds a man's sexual de-sire on specified occasions (*In 4 Sent.* 34,1,3).

We touch here upon another factor in the witch persecution, which was alluded to by Thorndike, namely, the tendency of theologians and inquisitors to interpret diseases, and especially mental disturbances, in demonic rather than in medical terms. In his *History of Medical Psychology* Gregory Zilboorg cites a pas-sage from the *Malleus*:

"Those err who say that there is no such thing as witchcraft but that it is purely imaginary, even although they do not believe that devils exist except in the imagination of the ignorant and vulgar, and the natural accidents which hap-pen to a man he wrongly attributes to some supposed devil. For the imagination of some men is so vivid that they think they see actual figures and appearances which are but the reflections of their thoughts, and then these are believed to be apparitions of evil spirits or even the specters of witches. But

[24] Hincmar, Epist. 22 (PL 126, 151). For other early documents dealing with this subject, see H. C. Lea, *Materials Toward a History of Witchcraft* (ed. A. C. Howland, New York 1957) I 162-70.
[25] *Decretales Gregorii* IX 4, 15 (*De frigidis et maleficiatis et impotentia coeundi*) Friedberg II 704-08.

62

this is contrary to [the] true faith which teaches us that certain angels fell from heaven and are now devils, and we are bound to acknowledge that by their very nature they can do many wonderful things which we cannot do. And those who try to induce others to perform such evil wonders are called witches. And because infidelity in a person who has been baptized is technically called heresy, therefore such persons are plainly heretics."

Zilboorg offers the following comment upon this statement:

This passage from the *Malleus* is perhaps the most significant statement to come out of the fifteenth century. Here, in a concise and succinct paragraph, two monks brush aside the whole mass of psychiatric knowledge which had been so carefully collected and preserved by almost two thousand years of medical and philosophic investigation; they brush it aside almost casually and with such stunning simplicity that no room is left for argument. How can one raise objections to the assertion, "but this is contrary to true faith"? The fusion of insanity, witchcraft, and heresy into one concept and the exclusion of even the suspicion that the problem is a medical one are now complete. It is no longer a matter of popular superstition; it is an authoritative principle of faith and law. Nothing may shake this dogma. No fact may be brought forth to cast a shadow on this principle.[26]

Unfortunately, Zilboorg was using Montague Summers' defective translation of the *Malleus,* which omits the attribution of the major part of the paragraph cited to St. Thomas. Thomas' strong condemnation of those who deny the existence of witches may have been directed against physicians, since it comes as a prologue to the analysis of bewitched impotency that we discussed above. Sprenger and Institoris add only the conclusion that infidelity is heresy. But at this point they are not saying that witchcraft is heresy, though they believe such to be the case, but

[26] G. Zilboorg and G. Henry, *A History of Medical Psychology* (New York 1941) 154-55.

that the denial of the existence of witchcraft is heresy. Zilboorg
is correct in his conclusion, however; the juggernaut of the witch-
hunt could only with great difficulty be opposed from within the
pale of orthodoxy.

4. The Critics of the Persecution

In view of the prevailing Catholic position on the subject of witchcraft, therefore, it is significant that the first effective resistance to
the witch mania came from a doctor who was also a heretic in
the eyes of the Catholics, namely, the Protestant Johann Wier
(or Weyer), the personal physician of the Duke of Cleves. We
have seen that St. Thomas could not visualize anyone denying
the existence of witchcraft without at the same time denying the
existence of demons. But in his *De praestigiis daemonum* ("The
Illusions of Demons"), which first appeared in 1563, Wier does
not go so far, but merely returns to the quasi-critical attitude
manifested in the *Episcopi eorumque* or more especially in St.
Augustine; that is, he does not deny any of the basic powers
attributed to demons but merely the claims made by or for most
witches. As D. P. Walker says:

Wier is still famous in our time, and was exceptional in
his own, for his disapproval of witch-burning; but this was
not because he believed magic and sorcery to be anything
but diabolic. Nearly all the operations of witchcraft were,
he thought, subjective delusions induced by evil demons.
Since the witches, being female and usually senile, were
too silly to be anything more than passive victims of the
Devil, they should not be so severely punished; the same leni-
ency should not be extended to male magicians, who often
voluntarily entered into commerce with demons. Though he
grudgingly concedes the possibility of good, natural magic,
he does in fact condemn all kinds of magical practices as involving demons and producing only illusory effects.[27]

[27] D. P. Walker, *Spiritual and Demonic Magic from Ficino to Campanella*
(Studies of the Warburg Institute 22, London 1958) 152-53.

64

He did, however, plead his case to a great extent precisely as a "heretic," that is to say, as a champion of new reforms. "Quite a large proportion of his treatise is directed not against secular magic but against Catholic practices and ceremonies which he regards as superstitious, and hence, at least potentially, demonic. These include most forms of exorcism, the use of the scriptures or the names of God or relics in curing diseases, the wearing of scriptural amulets, the baptism or consecration of bells and images." [28]

The same approach was used by Reginald Scot in England in his *Discovery of Witchcraft* (1584). He ridicules the "popish charms, conjurations, exorcisms, benedictions, and curses" of the papists. He says:

> They conjure water to be wholesome both for body and soul; but the body, we see, is never the better for it, nor the soul any whit reformed by it. And therefore I marvel that when they see their own conjurations confuted and brought to nought, or at least void of effect, that they, of all other, will yet give such credit, countenance, and authority to the vain cozenages of witches and conjurors, as though their charms and conjurations could produce more apparent, certain, and better effects than their own. [29]

Scot goes much further than Wier, for he starts from the Protestant principle that the age of miracles is over, and maintains that it holds good for wicked as well as holy people; just as saints are not aided by God to work miracles, so neither do witches effect wonders by the aid of demons. He even maintains that the evil spirits cannot interfere corporally with mankind, but only spiritually. We see in Genesis, for instance, how the devil came to "creep into the conscience of Eve, to abuse and deceive her." He did not take on the body of a serpent, but is simply called a serpent by way of metaphor. "And as for his corporal assaults, or his attempts

[28] *Ibid.* 153-54.
[29] Reginald Scot, *Discovery of Witchcraft* (London 1651) "Epistle to the Readers."

upon our bodies, his night walkings, his visible appearings, his dancing with witches, etc., we are neither warned in the scriptures of them, nor willed by God or his prophets to fly them, neither is there any mention made of them in the scriptures. And therefore think I those witchmongers and absurd writers to be as gross on the one side, as the Sadducees are impious and fond on the other, which say that spirits and devils are only motions and affections, and that angels are but tokens of God's power." [30]

Although Scot appeals to the writings of Calvin for support, his position, and even that of Wier, was too radical for most Reformers who joined the hunting of witches with a terrible zeal. Wier was refuted by the French Protestant lawyer Jean Bodin (whom Scot in turn attacked), and Wier and Scot together provoked the *Demonology* of King James I of Great Britain, who "almost certainly" ordered Scot's book to be burned by the common hangman.[31]

The policy of using extorted and unverified self-incrimination and of accepting prejudiced testimony and inadequate criteria, by means of which most of the witchcraft convictions were obtained, was a legal monstrosity, but it was centuries before the tribunals came to recognize the fact. In the early part of the seventeenth century one of the inquisitors who presided at witch trials in the Basque country, Alonso de Salazar y Frías, disagreed with the other judges, and in a minority report concluded that none of the alleged crimes upon which the convictions had been based had in fact been committed. The episode resembles the events that occurred in Salem, Massachusetts, at the end of the century. But the Salem incident was a kind of backwash that came after the tide of witch persecution had ebbed almost everywhere in Europe, whereas, when most of Salazar's ideas were incorporated in a memorandum on witchcraft published by the Supreme Tribunal of the Inquisition in Spain in 1614, it marked a new departure in the courts of Christendom.[32]

A few years later, a similar and, in a way, even more influential service was done by the German Jesuit Friedrich von Spee,

[30] *Ibid*, 8, 1 (p. 115); Appendix: "A Discourse upon evils and Spirits" c. 31 (pp. 386-87). Trevor-Roper (*op. cit.*) overlooks the crucial difference between the arguments of Wier and Scot.
[31] Wallace Notestein, *A History of Witchcraft in England from 1558 to 1718* (Washington 1911 repr. New York 1965) 69-70.
[32] Cf. Caro, *World* 184-89.

whose *Cautio criminalis* ("Caution in Criminal Proceedings") was published in 1631 without the authorization of his superiors and at the cost of serious opposition from within his order. His views on witchcraft resemble those of Wier's; that is, he was a moderate skeptic, but not one that denied all instances of diabolic witchcraft. His chief criticism of prevailing thought, however, lay in his refusal to accept the juridical abuses that had led to the condemnation of a vast number of innocent persons, many of whom he had assisted in their last moments before execution.[33]

For all practical purposes, the eighteenth century saw an end to legal prosecution of persons suspected of witchcraft; but belief in witchcraft can be found even at the present day, not only in the superstitions of the ignorant but also in the writings of Christian theologians who accept the basic demonological myths and theories inherited from the Fathers upon which the official concepts of witchcraft were based. In a recent work upon Spee, for instance, another Jesuit author finds that he can go no further than Spee on the theoretical level; the possibility of witchcraft cannot be denied, because the devil can work in perceptible ways in the world; for evidence, he cites the phenomena of diabolic possession.[34]

We shall see in the next chapter that ideas about possession have been built on just as frail a foundation as the theories of witchcraft. But as long as all these concepts are given dogmatic support in official circles, the fearsome machinery of the witch-hunt lies within reach, ready to be put into action wherever the faith of the people in these archaic doctrines can manage, at the bidding of fear and malevolence, to overcome their common sense.

---

[33] Cf. H. J. J. Zwetsloot, *Friedrich Spee und die Hexenprozesse; die Stellung und Bedeutung der Cautio criminalis in der Geschichte der Hexenverfolgungen* (Trier 1954); Emmy Rosenfeld, *Friedrich Spee von Langenfeld; eine Stimme in der Wüste* (Berlin 1958).
[34] Zwetsloot, *Friedrich Spee* 25.

IV
DEMONIC POSSESSION

In this chapter we will discuss diseases and other ailments thought to be caused by evil spirits. The most sensational of the afflictions ascribed to preternatural malice is demonic or diabolical possession, whereby a person's whole organism and personality seems to be under the control of an invading spirit, who can use even the victim's vocal organs to utter words or cries.

There is a close connection between demonic possession and witchcraft. This should be obvious, since we recall that witches were often accused of inflicting disease and injury upon men and animals through their demon assistants, and possession was also often thought to have been caused by sorcery. These notions are clearly seen in the *Roman Ritual,* the handbook of ceremonies and rites still used by Roman Catholic priests, the present form of which dates mostly from the early seventeenth century. In the instructions preceding the exorcisms currently prescribed for cases of possession there occurs the following directive, which was not touched in the 1952 revision of the rules: "Let him command the demon to say if he is kept in that body because of some magical practice or bewitching emblems or instruments; and if the possessed person has swallowed them, let him vomit them up; or if they should be somewhere else outside the body, let him reveal them; and when they are found they are to be burned." [1]

1. Jewish Traditions

In the Old Testament texts studied earlier there is little to suggest the notion of disease being caused by evil spirits, except per-

[1] *Rituale romanum* 12,1,20 (Turin 1952) 679-80.

67

haps for the seizures that Saul suffered from the evil spirit sent by Yahweh (1 Sam. 16, 14ff.). This spirit could sometimes be forced or persuaded to cease troubling the king when David played his lyre (1 Sam. 16, 23), but on other occasions the remedy seems to have had no effect, since Saul's reaction was to try to kill David (1 Sam. 18, 10-11; 19, 9-10).

We can recall too that the satan of the book of Job smites Job with boils from head to foot (Job 2, 7), but the affliction does not depend upon the continued presence of a spirit. Perhaps the noonday demon of the Septuagint is likewise visualized as a spirit that inflicts disease or death at midday.

There seems to be a similar conception in the book of Tobit; the demon Asmodeus apparently took up his abode in the bedroom of Sarah, where he would kill anyone who tried to take her to wife. Tobias, however, armed himself with the heart and liver of a fish at the suggestion of Raphael, who informed him that by burning these organs one could put an end to the molestations of any evil spirit and drive it away for good. Accordingly, we read that Asmodeus was baffled by the smell of the fish and ran away into upper Egypt where Raphael bound him in fetters, thus assuring his permanent removal.

In the New Testament, as we have seen, instances of demonic diseases are restricted to the synoptic authors. Since the synoptic gospels reflect a Galilean setting for the most part, it has been suggested that belief in possession was particularly strong in Galilee, whereas Judea was relatively free from it. According to Herbert Loewe, the Galilean and Babylonian rabbis almost invariably accepted, while the Judean rabbis rejected, the existence of evil spirits.[2] However this may be, it is true that John's gospel, which concentrates upon Judea, has no examples of demonic possession; but the charge of "having a demon" is occasionally leveled against Jesus (Jn. 7, 20; 8, 48; etc.). This expression however seems merely to have been a common way of calling someone's sanity into question.

In the Acts of the Apostles too there are episodes of exorcism and cure of demoniacs in areas far removed from Galilee, but this

---

[2] H. Loewe, "Demons and Spirits (Jewish)," *Encyclopedia of Religion and Ethics* 4,613.

book comes from the same tradition as the gospel of Luke. In Acts also we find perhaps the clearest statement of the synoptic tendency to attribute all illness to the devil. In one of the primitive *kerygmata* or summary sermons describing the mission of Jesus on earth, Peter says that "he went about doing good and healing all that were oppressed by the devil" (Acts 10, 38).

When we read of those who were healed during the course of Christ's sojourns in Galilee, we see that the maladies of some, like the lepers, are described simply in organic, not demonic, terms. But others are explicitly said to be the prey of unclean spirits or demons. These beings, as has been pointed out, are not to be confused with the devil himself, or to be interpreted as fallen angels.

The demons, however, seem to be ruled by the devil. This is the impression given by the episode in which the scribes explain Jesus' ministry by saying that "he is possessed by Beelzebul, and by the prince of demons he casts out the demons," since Jesus answers them by saying that Satan would not oppose himself in such a fashion (Mk. 3, 22-27).

In the gospel of Luke the connection between disease, demons, and the devil is strikingly presented. When Jesus heals Peter's mother-in-law he rebukes her fever just as he rebuked the demon of a possessed man earlier in the same day (Lk. 4, 33-39). When he appoints the seventy to go out and heal the sick, they come back rejoicing that even the demons are subject to them in his name, and he sees in their success the overthrow of Satan (Lk. 10, 9-20). Later there is described the woman who had a spirit (*pneuma*) of infirmity, and Jesus characterizes her affliction as a binding by Satan (Lk. 13, 11-16).

Jesus drives out the unclean spirits by his own authority, but his disciples, like the seventy, do it in his name. We recall that Paul ordered the pythonic spirit to depart out of a girl in the name of Jesus Christ (Acts 16, 18), and later we are told of a possessed man whose evil spirit resisted the attempt of some Jewish exorcists to adjure it "by the Jesus whom Paul preaches" (Acts 19, 11-16). However, even in Jesus' lifetime a man who was not a follower cast out demons in his name, and Jesus approved of his efforts (Mk. 8, 38-39).

It is interesting to note that Josephus speaks of a Jewish exorcist who successfully invoked Solomon's name in the cure of possession. He describes his method as follows:

> He put to the nose of the possessed man a ring which had under its seal one of the roots prescribed by Solomon, and then, as the man smelled it, drew out the demon through his nostrils, and, when the man at once fell down, adjured the demon never to come back into him, speaking Solomon's name and reciting the incantations which he had composed.[3]

Justin believed it impossible for demons to be driven out in the name of any person but God, and in his conversation with Trypho he argues that the efficacy of the name of Jesus against demons proves that he is the Lord of hosts. He says:

> For every demon when exorcized in the name of this very Son of God . . . is overcome and subdued. But though you exorcize any demon in the name of any of those who were amongst you—either kings, or righteous men, or prophets or patriarchs—it will not be subject to you. But if any of you exorcize it in the name of the God of Abraham and the God of Isaac and the God of Jacob, it will perhaps be subject to you. Now assuredly your exorcists, I have said, make use of craft (*techne*) when they exorcize, even as the Gentiles do, and employ fumigations and incantations (*katadesmoi,* "bonds"). (*Dial.* 85 ANF)

2. The Practice of the Early Christians

It is difficult to determine from the above passage what Justin's opinion was about the success of Jewish exorcists who used the name of God. But his witness to the effectiveness of Christian exorcists is clear and insistent. We have already referred to his argument that the successes they achieved were proof of the truth of Christianity. He is speaking to the Romans:

[3] Josephus, *Jewish Antiquities* 8, 2, 5 Loeb.

For numberless demoniacs throughout the whole world, and
in your city, many of our Christian men exorcizing them
in the name of Jesus Christ, who was crucified under Pontius
Pilate, have healed and do heal, rendering helpless and driving the possessing demons out of the men, though they
could not be cured by all the other exorcists, and those who
used incantations and drugs (*2 Apol.* 6).

T. K. Oesterreich says of this claim:

It seems, indeed, that this was not a matter of mere personal
conviction, but was really the case; the Christian exorcists
were able to record the greatest successes, because they an-
swered best to those requirements which we have learned to
recognize as necessary to the success of exorcism. The Christians possessed absolute certainty of victory, founded on their
faith in Christ. To this was added the high moral value of their
doctrine, which opened to them the hearts of the sick and the
oppressed. That deliverance from all the burdens of the soul
which the modern man experiences when he enters a circle
of true believers in Jesus must have occurred in a far higher
degree amongst the Christians of the two first generations
to whom the memory of Christ was still a living thing. Men
were alive who had known him, or their sayings had been
heard by the ears of those present, and to this must be added
the belief in his imminent second coming. It is difficult for us
to conceive any idea of the conviction and exaltation of
these early Christians. How strong their influence must have
been, when their religion was still young, their faith still fresh
and vivid, not yet overlaid with the grey dust of two thousand years of dogmatics! The great success of the Christian exorcists is therefore readily understood, and its reality is
attested by the fact that other exorcists who were not true
Christians, and even certain Jews, likewise uttered conjurations
in the name of Jesus.[4]

[4] T. K. Oesterreich, *Possession, Demoniacal and Other; among Primitive
Races, in Antiquity, the Middle Ages, and Modern Times* (tr. D. Ibberson,
London 1930) 165.

Daniélou notes that the early Christians attributed the power of Jesus' name over demons to his passion on the cross, and reference to his passion became a part of the formulas of exorcism.[5] This practice is reflected in the words of Justin, and we have seen another example of it in the cure of the maniac related by Epiphanius in his *Panarion* (30, 10). In the same episode we saw that water signed with the cross was sprinkled over the patient while the words of adjuration were spoken. In Jewish tradition there is recorded a story that attributed to pagan exorcism the use of sprinkled water. In the *Midrash Rabbah* it is related of Rabbi Johanan ben Zakkai, who lived in the first century A.D., that an idolator asked him for an explanation of various Hebrew rituals, which seemed to him a kind of witchcraft. The rabbi asked him what their own practice was in dealing with a man possessed by the demon of madness. " 'We bring roots,' he replied, 'and make them smoke under him, then we sprinkle water upon the demon and it flees.' " Rabbi Johanan told him that there was a similar explanation for their ritual washings—water of purification was sprinkled upon the unclean, and the unclean spirit would flee. But when the idolater had departed the rabbi made it clear that he had merely put him off with a makeshift explanation that he could understand. In reality the rite had no exorcistic function at all, and the sole reason for it was that God had commanded it.[6]

We have seen that in the exorcistic or apotropaic rites preceding baptism in the Valentinian gnostic sect to which Theodotus belonged in the middle of the second century, use was made of fasts, prayers, impositions of hands, and genuflections. In the gospels, Jesus is ordinarily described as driving out demons by a simple command, though he lays his hands on the women bound by Satan with a spirit of infirmity (Lk. 13, 13); the laying on of hands is also his general method of curing which at times seems to have included the expelling of demons (Lk. 4, 40-41). In one of the Dead Sea scrolls, the *Genesis Apocryphon,* Abraham is pictured as

[5] J. Daniélou, "Exorcisme," *Dictionnaire de spiritualité* 4 (1960) 1997.
[6] *Numbers Rabbah* 19, 8 (*Midrash Rabbah* 6, tr. J. J. Slotki, London 1961) 757-58; cf. R. J. Zwi Werblowsky, "On the Baptismal Rite According to St. Hippolytus," *Studia patristica* 2 (ed. K. Aland and F. L. Cross, Texte und Untersuchungen 64, Berlin 1957) 104-05.

driving away an evil spirit from the pharaoh by the imposition of hands and the invocation of God (20, 29); [7] and in the Acts of the Apostles it is said that the sick were cured of sicknesses and evil spirits by having articles of Paul's clothing placed upon them (Acts 19, 12).

There was, of course, nothing necessarily exorcistic in the imposition of hands, or prayer and fasting. We observe, for instance, that prayer, fasting, and the imposition of hands made up the rite of ordination described in the Acts of the Apostles (13, 3). It is difficult to know when fasting was brought into play as an element in Christian exorcism, since its mention in the gospels, where Jesus speaks of a kind of spirit that will depart only through prayer and fasting (Mk. 9, 29; Mt. 17, 21), is most probably a later interpolation.[8]

At the beginning of the third century other features of Christian exorcism appear. Tertullian remarks in his *Apology* (c. 23) that "the wicked spirit, bidden to speak by a follower of Christ, will as readily make the truthful confession that he is a demon, as elsewhere he has falsely asserted that he is a god" (ANF). This notion that the evil spirits when properly adjured must tell the truth or obey appears often in later times. It may have had Jewish antecedents, to judge from a passage in the *Philopseudes* or "Lover of Lies" of the second-century Syrian satirist Lucian. A credulous character named Ion says:

I should like to ask you what you say to those who free possessed men from their terrors by exorcizing the spirits so manifestly. I need not discuss this; everyone knows about the Syrian from Palestine, the adept in it, how many he takes in hand who fall down in the light of the moon and roll their eyes and fill their mouths with foam; nevertheless, he restores them to health and sends them away normal in mind, delivering them from their straits for a large fee. When he stands beside them as they lie there and asks:

[7] *The Genesis Apocryphon of Qumran Cave I* (ed. J. A. Fitzmyer, Biblica et orientalia 18, Rome 1966) 58-59.
[8] See Herbert Musurillo, "The Problem of Ascetical Fasting in the Greek Patristic Writers," *Traditio* 12 (1956) 21 n. 16 and 46 n. 20.

74

"Whence came you into his body?" the patient himself is silent, but the spirit (*daimon*) answers in Greek or in the language of whatever foreign country he comes from, telling how and whence he entered into the man; whereupon, by adjuring the spirit and, if he does not obey, threatening him, he drives him out. Indeed, I actually saw one coming out, black and smoky in color (c. 16 Loeb).

Lucian obviously did not credit all the details of this story, but some of his contemporaries no doubt did believe them, and the account must have had some basis in reality.

Lucian's Palestinian exorcist is said to have threatened the more recalcitrant demons; this technique became common in Christian exorcism as well, where the usual threat was an increase in their eternal punishment. We see something of this already in Tertullian, according to whom the mere reminder of the demons' future fate suffices:

All the authority and power we have over them is from our naming the name of Christ, and recalling to their memory the woes with which God threatens them at the hands of Christ as judge, and which they expect one day to overtake them. Fearing Christ in God, and God in Christ, they become subject to the servants of God and Christ. So at our touch and breathing, overwhelmed by the thought and realization of those judgment fires, they leave at our command the bodies they have entered, unwilling and distressed, and before your very eyes put to an open shame (*Apol.* 23).

He alludes here to the practice of breathing upon the possessed person. This act became a feature of later exorcisms, especially in several baptismal rituals.

Minucius Felix, who also wrote in Africa about the same time as Tertullian, speaks as if the words of exorcism themselves inflicted pain upon the demons.[9] The same idea is expressed later in

[9] Minucius Felix, *Octavius* 27; on Minucius as an African, see Wolfgang Speyer, "Octavius, der Dialog des Minucius Felix: Fiktion oder historische Wirklichkeit?" *Jahrbuch für Antike und Christentum* 7 (1964) 45-51.

the third century by Cyprian, another African: "Oh, would you but hear and see them when they are adjured by us, and tortured with spiritual scourges, and are ejected from the possessed bodies with tortures of words, when howling and groaning at the voice of man and the power of God, feeling the stripes and blows, they confess the judgment to come!" (*To Demetrianus* 15 ANF).

The influence of demons and the operations of the exorcists were extended to specific locales (like haunted houses) and to animals as well as to the bodies of men. Origen writes: "For ourselves, so far are we from wishing to serve demons, that by the use of prayers and other means which we learn from scripture, we drive them out of the souls of men, out of places where they have established themselves, and even sometimes from the bodies of animals; for even these creatures often suffer from injuries inflicted upon them by demons" (*Against Celsus* 7, 67 ANF). St. Jerome, in his *Life of St. Hilarion* written towards the end of the fourth century, describes at length how the celebrated ascetic delivered an enormous camel from the devil (c. 23).

Jerome's work is an example of a body of literature that might be termed the "Tall Tales from the Desert Series," represented more famously by Athanasius' *Life of St. Antony* and continued in the *Conferences* of John Cassian. Legendary material of an extreme naiveté was incorporated into these writings and passed on in the hopes of edifying the faithful. The same policy was followed by Gregory the Great late in the sixth century in his *Dialogues*. We read there, for instance:

On a certain day a servant of God from the aforesaid monastery of virgins entered the garden, and saw a head of lettuce that she desired; and forgetting to bless it with the sign of the cross she greedily bit into it. All at once, however, she was seized by the devil and fell to the ground. As she was being tormented word was quickly brought to the beforementioned father Equitius so that he might come at once to her aid with his prayers. Soon after, when the said father had entered the garden, the devil who had seized her began to cry out from her mouth, as if to justify himself, saying, "What did I do? What did I do? I was sitting on the lettuce—she

came along and bit me!" With grave indignation the man of
God ordered him to go out and keep no place in the servant
of almighty God. He departed at once, and could not manage
to come upon her again. (1,4) [10]

This account may be a perfectly accurate report of an actual incident. The naiveté consists in giving credit to the demonological
fantasies of the nun.

It was this sort of popular hagiographical and homiletic tradition that was to keep alive the notions of possession that have
survived up to the present time. In Jerome's *Hilarion,* for example,
we have a case described precisely like the one envisaged by
the *Roman Ritual* in the rule quoted at the beginning of this
chapter. A youth who fell in love with a girl made no progress
by the ordinary means of seduction, and so he studied other methods for a year with a magician at Memphis. When he came back,
he

> buried beneath the threshold of the girl's house certain magi-
> cal formulae and revolting figures engraven on a plate of
> Cyprian brass. Thereupon the maid began to show signs of in-
> sanity, to throw away the covering of her head, tear her hair,
> gnash her teeth, and loudly call the youth by name. Her in-
> tense affection had become a frenzy. Her parents therefore
> brought her to the monastery and delivered her to the aged
> saint. No sooner was this done than the devil began to howl
> and confess. "I was compelled, I was carried off against my
> will. How happy I was when I used to beguile the men of
> Memphis in their dreams! What crosses, what tortures I suffer!
> You force me to go out, and I am kept bound under the
> threshold. I cannot go out unless the young man who keeps
> me there lets me go."

Hilarion, however, had less faith in the power of magic than the
authors of the *Roman Ritual*:

> But the saint would not command search to be made for

10 PL 77, 168-69.

either the young man or the charms till the maiden had
undergone a process of purgation, for fear that it might be
thought that the demon had been released by means of incantations, or that he himself had attached credit to what he
said. He declared that demons are deceitful and well versed
in dissimulation, and sharply rebuked the virgin when she
had recovered her health for having by her conduct given
an opportunity for the demon to enter. (c. 21 NPNF)

In the next chapter another demoniac enters the picture and we
get an early example of the preternatural feats later regarded as
decisive in establishing specific cases of demonic possession.
The episode stresses especially xenoglossia, that is, the knowledge of foreign tongues, a phenomenon noticed also by the character in Lucian's dialogue. Jerome's account reads:

Immediately on being questioned by the servant of God the
man sprang up on tiptoe, so as scarcely to touch the ground
with his feet, and with a wild roar replied in Syriac, in which
language he had been interrogated. Pure Syriac was heard
flowing from the lips of a barbarian who knew only French
and Latin, and that without the absence of a sibilant or an
aspirate or an idiom of the speech of Palestine.

3. The Evolution of the Exorcist

The casting out of demons was one of the features of the apostolic commission as handed down in Mark (16, 17), and, like other
forms of instantaneous curing, was regarded in the early Church
as one of the miraculous powers by which Christians were able to
manifest the glory of God. The power of performing these marvelous deeds was not conferred by ordination but was considered
a charism imparted directly by God.

When, however, the theory of the ethical demonic possession
of the unbaptized inspired the practice of prebaptismal exorcism,
it became necessary to have the exorcisms performed by regularly
appointed officials rather than to rely on the presence of charis-

matic individuals. In the *Apostolic Tradition* of Hippolytus, which dates from early third-century Rome, it is directed that hands be placed on the candidates daily while they are exorcized (c. 20).[11] It does not say who performs the exorcisms, although previously it specifies that the person instructing the catechumens, whether he is a cleric (*ekklesiastikos*) or layman, is to place his hands over them and pray before dismissing them (c. 19). Towards the end of their training program the bishop himself is to exorcize the candidates in order to see if they are clean. "If one is not virtuous or clean, he is to be set aside, because he has not heard the word in faith, for it is impossible for the alien one always to remain hidden" (c. 20).

Examples of people whom Hippolytus considers unclean and therefore not eligible for baptism are prostitutes, inverts, and eunuchs, as well as magicians, diviners, and so forth (c. 16). Furthermore, if anyone has a demon, he is not to attend instructions until he is clean (c. 15). It is not specified how such a one is made clean, or how his state is different from the other candidates, since it is said that on Holy Saturday "the bishop is to place his hand on them and exorcize all alien spirits so that they may flee from them and not return into them" (c. 20). Presumably, however, the one who has a demon is agitated by him in a visible way, and is the kind of demoniac traditionally cured by the charismatic exorcist. It is noteworthy that Hippolytus specified earlier that those with the power of healing are not to be ordained: "If anyone says, 'I have received the grace of healing in a revelation,' he is not to have the hand laid on him; for the outcome itself will show whether he is speaking the truth" (c. 14).

In the middle of the third century, Pope Cornelius in a letter preserved by Eusebius mentions exorcists as one of the orders of the clergy at Rome.[12] There is no indication of their function, whether they assisted at baptism or attempted the cure of the violently possessed, or both. They are still found there at the be-

---

[11] *La Tradition apostolique de saint Hippolyte* (ed. B. Botte, Münster 1963) 42.

[12] Eusebius, *Ecclesiastical History* 6, 43, 11, GCS 9, 618. This is the usual interpretation of the pope's statement but F. Claeys Bouuaert, "Exorciste," *Dictionnaire de droit canonique* 5 (1953) 672-73, points out that it does not actually say that they were ordained.

ginning of the sixth century but it was not obligatory for the clergy to pass through that degree of the hierarchy, and several decades later it was almost extinct. Michel Andrieu finds it significant that in the prebaptismal ceremonies of *Ordo romanus XI,* which dates from the second half of the sixth or the beginning of the seventh century, it is acolytes or priests who say the exorcisms.[13] In Gaul, however, the exorcist maintained a more uninterrupted tradition. In the last half of the fifth century a set of canons was composed, perhaps by Gennadius of Marseilles, called *Statuta ecclesiae antiqua* ("Ancient Statutes of the Church") and regularly ascribed to a Fourth Council of Carthage;[14] they directed the exorcists to lay their hands daily on the energumens (those agitated by demons) and to feed them regularly in the house of God; the energumens in turn are to sweep out the houses of God (cc. 62-64). The *Statuta* has this canon on the ordination of exorcists: "When the exorcist is ordained, let him receive from the hand of the bishop the book in which the exorcisms are written, while the bishop says to him, 'Receive and memorize it, and possess the power of laying hands on the energumen, whether baptized or catechumen' " (c. 95).

This canon was incorporated into the Gallican liturgical books and brought to Rome in the tenth century, when the exorcist again became one of the ranks through which clerics had to pass before receiving major orders.[15] Accordingly, it found its way into Gratian's *Decretum* (1,23,17). It will be noticed that the canon visualizes the activity of the exorcist as limited to the helping of energumens. But one manuscript tradition of the *Statuta,* originating in Spain in the seventh century and found in Italy in the eighth, extends the exorcist's function to the prebaptismal services by specifying that he is to lay hands "on energumens or on those who are to be baptized."[16]

In the Eastern Church in early times a number of different

---

[13] M. Andrieu, *Les Ordines romani du haut moyen âge* 3 (Louvain 1951) 543-44; 4 (1956) 23-24.

[14] *Statuta ecclesiae antiqua,* ed. C. Munier, *Concilia Galliae, A. 314-A. 506* (Corpus christianorum, series latina 148, Turnhout 1963) 162-88.

[15] Andrieu, *Ordines* 3, 572-73. 596-97; 4, 24.

[16] Andrieu took this reading to be the original in his edition of this part of the *Statuta* (*Ordines* 3,618).

practices are found. The liturgies of Jerusalem, Antioch, and Mopsuestia in the fourth and fifth centuries employ exorcists in the prebaptismal ceremonies, but in later liturgies of these areas and of Greece such ceremonies are performed by other ministers, a development paralleling the one that Andrieu conjectures for Rome.

In the *Apostolic Constitutions,* a pseudepigraphous body of directives that may reflect the liturgy of Cyrrhus in West Syria in the first half of the fifth century,[17] there are no baptismal exorcisms, even though the author draws on the *Apostolic Tradition.* There is, however, a section on exorcists, that is, those who have the charism of curing illnesses, who, as in the *Tradition,* are not ordained but are chosen directly by God's grace (8,26,2).[18] There are also special prayers in the eucharistic liturgy recited by the deacon and bishop on behalf of the energumens (8,7,2-4; 8,12,47). A century later another Syrian or Palestinian pseudonymous document, the *Ecclesiastical Hierarchy* of Pseudo-Dionysius the Areopagite,[19] also describes a class of energumens, who like the catechumens and penitents are not allowed to participate in the mysteries (3,3,7); however, there is no mention of exorcists who effect their cure, nor for that matter any indication that it is demons who cause their disturbances; blame is placed upon their pusillanimity and uncontrolled imagination, and they are urged to overcome their groundless fears.

If there was a custom of ordaining exorcists anywhere in the East, it eventually died out. At the Fourth Council of Constantinople (A.D. 869-70), computed as the eighth ecumenical, which was convoked against Photius, the rank of lector was the only minor order specified as a necessary preliminary to becoming a bishop (10,5).[20] In general, the Eastern churches have resisted Roman pressure to accept the obsolete minor orders as they exist in the

[17] Cf. J. Ysebaert, *Greek Baptismal Terminology; Its Origins and Early Development* (Graecitas christianorum primaeva 1, Nijmegen 1962) 317-18.

[18] Ed. F. X. Funk, *Didascalia et Constitutiones apostolorum* (Paderborn 1905).

[19] Ed. Johannes Quasten, *Monumenta eucharistica et liturgica vetustissima* (Florilegium patristicum 7, Bonn 1935-37) 275-328.

[20] G. D. Mansi, *Sacra concilia* 16 (Venice 1771) 401.

West. For one example, Innocent IV in the thirteenth century unsuccessfully demanded that the Greeks accept the four Latin minor orders.[21] The Armenian Church was an exception; in the Middle Ages, under the influence of the crusaders, it incorporated an order of exorcist, conceived as a minister who read the exorcisms at baptism.[22]

The Second Vatican Council's *Decree on the Eastern Catholic Churches* might seem to give the impression at one point that it is urging the various Eastern rites to adopt the Latin minor orders.[23] In fact, however, it is currently being proposed that the Latin rite abandon the orders of porter, acolyte, and exorcist.

4. The Church and Demoniacs in the Middle Ages and Later

Although the Eastern branches of the Church do not have an order of exorcist, the tradition of demonic illness has survived among them in various forms. In the ritual of the Byzantine rite there are a number of long exorcisms, attributed to Saints Basil the Great and John Chrysostom, to be recited over those believed to be possessed by the devil. In some of the prayers God is addressed and asked to intervene; but in others the devil himself is berated, sometimes with a repetition of formulas that has an incantatory effect.[24] They describe at length the kind of activity the evil spirit is thought to undertake. However, in the one ceremony in which a ritual action is called for (the patient is to be anointed with oil), there is no explicit mention of the devil or demons, in spite of the title of the service: "Office of prayer for sick persons agitated by unclean and possessing spirits." [25]

[21] Innocent IV, *Sub catholicae professione* 19 (6 March 1254) ES 836.
[22] *Ordinationes armenorum: ordinatio exorcistae,* in H. Denziger, *Ritus orientalium, coptorum, syrorum, et armenorum, in administrandis sacramentis* 2 (Würzburg 1864) 280-81.
[23] The decree reads (n. 17): "The legislative authority of each individual church should decide about the subdiaconate and the minor orders, including their rights and obligations." *The Documents of Vatican II* (ed. Walter M. Abbott, New York 1966) 380-81.
[24] *Euchologion sive rituale graecorum,* ed. Jacques Goar (2 ed. Venice 1730 repr. Graz 1960) 578-85, esp. 583.
[25] *Ibid.* 575-78.

As for the Church in the West, we saw that the fifth-century *Statuta ecclesiae antiqua* referred to a book of exorcisms to be used on the energumens. Unfortunately no such book has come down to us. Most of the exorcisms for the possessed collected in the *Roman Ritual* are based on baptismal exorcisms. According to Adolphe Franz, the earliest demonstrable ecclesiastical exorcism formulas for the possessed go back only to the seventh and eighth centuries.[26] The first one he lists appears in the *Old Gallican Missal,* in a manuscript dating from the beginning of the eighth century. It is significant that it is included in the missal as a pre-baptismal exorcism. It reads:

I come against you, most unclean damned spirit; you are grown old in evil, the substance of crimes, the origin of sin; you delight in deceits, sacrileges, defilements, slaughters. Invoking the name of our Lord Jesus Christ we rebuke you and adjure you through his majesty and power, passion and resurrection, advent and judgment, that in whatever part of the members you are hiding, you manifest yourself by your own confession, and that, shaken by spiritual flames and invisible torments, you flee from the vessel that you believe yourself in possession of, leaving it purged for the Lord after having been your dwelling-place. Let it suffice that in former ages you ruled over almost the whole of the world in the hearts of men. Now day by day your kingdom will be destroyed, and may your weapons daily grow ineffectual until the end. What you suffer now was long ago prefigured. Already you were devastated by the plagues of the Egyptians, you were drowned in the Pharaoh, destroyed in Jericho, prostrated in the seven Chanaanite nations, defeated by Samson in the Philistines, cut off by David in Goliath, hanged by Mordecai in Haman, cast down by Daniel in Bel, punished in the dragon, pierced through by Judith in Holofernes, subjugated by the Lord to human commands, blinded by Paul in the magician, burned in the serpent, burst open by Peter in Simon; by all the saints you are put to rout, tortured, lacerated, con-

---

[26] A. Franz, *Die kirchlichen Benediktionen im Mittelalter* (Freiburg im Breisgau 1909) II 579.

signed to eternal fires and infernal darkness, from where our Lord Jesus Christ as a second Adam rescues man while he triumphs over you. Depart, depart, wherever you are, and seek no more to enter bodies dedicated to God. May they be forbidden to you forever, in the name of the Father and Son and Holy Spirit, and in the glory of the Lord's passion, by whose blood they are saved, whose advent they await, whose judgment they confess.[27]

Whatever function ordained exorcists might have had in attempting the cure of demoniacs in the Western Church, this task, as in the case of the baptismal exorcisms, was eventually assumed by clerics of higher orders. For instance, in the Gallican liturgy formerly followed by the Church in Spain there is a solemn rite of exorcism dating from the eleventh century or earlier, in which the afflicted person is brought into church and placed before the altar, while the clergy group into two choirs and respond to prayers chanted by a deacon and by the bishop or senior priest.[28] The priest became the normal minister in the exorcizing of demoniacs and thus the rites are contained in the priest's manual, the *Roman Ritual*. But not until the time of Pius XI in the 20th century did the *Ritual* specifically limit the exercise of the office to priests and omit mention of "other exorcists" and "other legitimate ministers." [29]

At the time of the Reformation, exorcism of the possessed began to function somewhat as it did in the early Church, when success in curing demoniacs was taken as a proof of the truth of Christianity. Catholics especially regarded this ability as a divine sign of their orthodoxy, and the alleged failure of the Protestants was seen as an indication of divine displeasure with their heresies.

We have seen that the Reformers soon became dissatisfied with many of the assumptions that lay behind exorcism, especially when it was a matter of exorcizing material elements. As we

---

[27] *Missale gallicanum vetus* 13 (ed. L. C. Mohlberg, Rerum ecclesiasticarum documenta, series maior, fontes 3, Rome 1958) 17.

[28] *Le Liber ordinum en usage dans l'Église wisigothique et mozarabe d'Espagne du cinquième au onzième siècle* 26 (ed. M. Férotin, Monumenta ecclesiae liturgica 5, Paris 1904) 73-80. As a prebaptismal rite this service is found, at least in part, in the seventh century.

[29] Claeys Bouuaert, "Exorciste" 675.

have said, the Lutherans at first retained certain baptismal exorcisms and practiced exorcism over demoniacs; it was not until the end of the sixteenth century that a movement began to discard it as superstition. The Calvinists did away with all exorcism, believing it to have been valid only in the early Church. In England exorcism was practiced on both sides of the establishment, by Puritans and by Jesuits. The Catholic exorcists were attacked by Samuel Harsnett (later archbishop of York) in *A Declaration of Egregious Popish Impostures* (1603), and the 1604 Convocation passed a canon "which forbids any Anglican clergyman, without the express consent of his bishop obtained beforehand, to use exorcism in any fashion under any pretext, on pain of being counted an impostor and deposed from the ministry." [30]

In the Roman Catholic Church, similar but less decisive measures were eventually taken. In the *Roman Ritual,* issued in 1614 under Paul V, the following rule for the exorcist appears:

First of all he should not easily believe that anyone is possessed by a demon, but let him know the signs whereby a possessed person can be distinguished from those who suffer from black bile [melancholy] or some disease. Now the signs of a possessing demon are: the speaking of many words or the understanding of a speaker in an unknown tongue; the revealing of distant and occult things; the manifestation of powers beyond the nature of one's age or condition; and other things of this sort, which when several occur together are all the more decisive indications.[31]

This precaution greatly diminished the practice of exorcism. Furthermore, many local diocesan and provincial synods passed laws requiring episcopal permission for exorcism, as the Church of England did in 1604. Several directives from Rome during the eighteenth century require this restriction for certain specified dioceses. These documents are cited as the sources for the canon ex-

---

[30] Wallace Notestein, *A History of Witchcraft in England* 87-88.
[31] *Rituale romanum* 12, 1, 3. In 1952 the wording of this rule was changed to read: ". . . who suffer from some disease, especially those caused by psychic factors. . . the signs of a possessing demon can be . . ." Cf. Corrado Balducci, *Gli indemoniati* (Rome 1959) 391. 423.

tending the rule to the whole of the Latin Church in 1917. The canon reads:

> No one who has the power of exorcism can legitimately exercise it upon the possessed unless he has obtained the special and explicit permission of his ordinary.
>
> This permission will be granted by the ordinary only to a priest endowed with piety and prudence, and of upright life; he is not to proceed with the exorcisms until a diligent and prudent investigation reveals that the person to be exorcised is really possessed by a demon.[32]

These rules have helped immensely to lower the number of suspected possessions, but the concept remains alive. This is the case even in the Church of England, where, in the 1958 Convocation of Canterbury, it was strongly affirmed; and at the same time a suggestion that the doctrinal status of belief in the devil be investigated was decisively voted down.

5. Modern Views of Possession

As early as the sixteenth century, as we saw when discussing Reginald Scot, the existence of diabolical possession was denied. In 1599 Samuel Harsnett, who was influenced by Scot, wrote in his *Discovery of the Fraudulent Practices of John Darrel* (Darrel was a Puritan exorcist): "Whether witches can send devils into men and women (as many do pretend) is a question amongst those that write of such matters, and the learneder and sounder sort do hold the negative." [33]

In the next century Thomas Hobbes, in the fourth book of the *Leviathan,* moved against the existence of the demons themselves. He noted that just as God's direct address to the light and other creatures in the Genesis narrative of creation did not imply intelligence in them, so too Christ's addressing demons in sick persons did not mean that such spirits really possessed them; and he

---

[32] *Codex iuris canonici* 1151 (Ed. P. Gasparri, Vatican 1963) 385-86.
[33] Cited in Notestein, *Witchcraft in England* 90 n. 41.

corroborated this position by pointing out that Jesus used the same word of rebuke against both demons and inanimate forces like the wind and waves.

Oesterreich describes the attack made upon the concept of demonic possession by Protestant theologians in Germany beginning with Johann Solomon Semler in the eighteenth century. And though he admits that belief in possession is not entirely extinct in Protestantism, he still feels that by the nineteenth century it had received its deathblow; however, he adds, "the demonological theory of primitive Christian times is immutably perpetuated by the Catholic Church." But there is one other environment in civilized countries where states of possession are freely manifested, and that is among spiritualists.[34]

By "states of possession" Oesterreich means symptoms that make it appear that a person has been invaded by an alien personality. The nature of this added personality is determined by the beliefs of the patient. In the case of a traditional Christian, it normally manifests the characteristics of a Christian demon, that is, the kind of evil spirit evolved in Christian thought over the ages. In the case of a spiritualist medium, it will be one of the spirits of the departed.

Oesterreich divides such states of possession into two main forms, the paroxysmal (with somnambulistic or trance-like states) and the lucid. This analysis is followed even by writers who believe in the existence of genuine diabolical possession, when they are describing conditions that they admit to be possession only in appearance. This is true, for example, of the Catholic neurologist Jean Lhermitte in his work on *Diabolical Possession, True and False*. It is interesting to note that the only examples he gives of true possession are the demoniacs of the gospels.

Lhermitte classifies under the paroxysmal form of pseudo-possession certain kinds of epileptic attacks, psychoneuroses, and hysteria; under special conditions hysteria can result in epidemics of possession, that is, in a whole series of convulsionaries, as happened in the case of the Ursulines of Loudun in the seventeenth century. In all these forms, the normal personality alternates with that of the "demon," though these personalities are not entirely unaware of each other. But in the lucid form of possession,

[34] Oesterreich, *Possession* 192-94. 199. 202.

"the demoniacal control is permanent. While they speak to you, these patients have no doubt that they are penetrated by the evil spirit. So in the same mind there coexist two personalities who hate and fight each other bitterly." [35]

We have seen the warning of the *Roman Ritual* to exorcists to make certain that a person is really possessed and not afflicted by a natural ailment. F. X. Maquart cites a similar warning issued in the sixteenth century by the National Synod of Rheims (1583), and alludes to the work of the Jesuit theologian Petrus Thyräus at the end of the century, who "rejects twelve of the accepted signs of possession as unreliable, in spite of all opinions to the contrary." [36]

Maquart attempts to bring the criteria for determining genuine possession up to date. He starts with the supposition that the Christian faith demands belief in demons, which he assumes to be the fallen angels of patristic tradition interpreted as the pure spirits of Thomistic philosophy. He believes that when such spirits interfere drastically with the body and personality of a human being the resulting actions will take on a superhuman quality that can accurately expose them for what they are. It is only then, in accordance with the regulation of the *Roman Ritual,* that exorcism should be commenced.

He admits the possibility that a demon might be simulating the symptoms of a natural affliction, thus disguising his presence and avoiding the rigors of being exposed to the spiritual assaults of exorcism. But he neither poses nor answers the question why evil spirits, who supposedly possess a high order of intelligence, would ever make the mistake of laying themselves open to expulsion by performing indiscreet wonders.

Adolf Rodewyk attempts to give a solution to this dilemma by the use of what he calls probative exorcism, prayers of exorcism that do not need episcopal permission as does solemn exorcism. These prayers are to be recited silently in the presence of the suspected victim of possession (an audible recitation might provoke a purely hysterical simulation of possession), and if the subject

[35] J. Lhermitte, *Diabolical Possession, True and False* (tr. P. J. Hepbourne-Scott, London 1963) 91.
[36] F. X. Maquart, "Exorcism and Diabolical Manifestation," *Satan* (New York 1952) 180. 192-94.

reacts with insults, blasphemy, and so on, it will help to confirm the diagnosis of possession. However, Rodewyk's views upon this subject are contradictory. At one point he admits the possibility that even in such a test the devil will do nothing out of the ordinary, attempting to disguise his presence as long as possible. On the next page, however, he says that, although preternatural events can occur apart from exorcism, when exorcism is used they must inevitably occur if there is true possession, and herein, he says, lies the importance of probative exorcism.[37] This idea hearkens back to Tertullian's notion that when adjured by a Christian the demons must tell the truth. But even when solemn exorcism is performed, according to Rodewyk, it can have varying degrees of success, or lack of success, depending on the circumstances.[38] Finally, the possibility of telepathy or other non-demonic paranormal powers of perception, which Rodewyk stresses elsewhere in an attempt to define the preternatural, would seem largely to invalidate his claims for the usefulness of probative exorcism.

The question remains whether such marvelous phenomena as those that Maquart and Rodewyk demand for authenticating a possession have ever occurred. The test of knowledge of a foreign language, singled out by the *Roman Ritual,* has received much attention from writers on possession; but it appears that unambiguous instances of it have never really been established. Aldous Huxley says in this regard:

In the cases where persons in a state of trance have shown an unequivocal knowledge of some language of which they were consciously ignorant, investigation has generally revealed the fact that they had spoken the language during childhood and subsequently forgotten it, or that they had heard it spoken and, without understanding the meaning of the words had unconsciously familiarized themselves with their sound. For the rest there is, in the words of F. W. H. Myers, "little evidence of the acquisition—telepathy apart—of

[37] A. Rodewyk, *Die dämonische Besessenheit in der Sicht des Rituale romanum* (Zürich 1963) 68-69.
[38] *Ibid.* 66-67.

any actual mass of fresh knowledge, such as a new language, or a stage of mathematical knowledge unreached before." [39] In the light of what we know, through systematic psychical research, of trance mediumship and automatic writing, it seems questionable whether any alleged demoniac ever passed the test of language in a completely unambiguous and decided manner. What is certain is that the recorded cases of complete failure are very numerous, while the recorded successes are mostly partial and rather unconvincing.[40]

Corrado Balducci, a champion of the Western Catholic traditions of possession and exorcism, has recently written a six-hundred-page book on the subject. While he exhibits the same simple and undisturbed faith as Maquart in the concepts of medieval theology and philosophy concerning the nature of demons, he shows a good deal of critical acumen in evaluating the claims of various preternatural phenomena. Specifically, he agrees with Huxley that the wonder of xenoglossia has never been satisfactorily demonstrated. But he opposes Maquart's view that preternatural phenomena are necessary to establish true possession, or that the *Roman Ritual* requires such proof; it is sufficient, he maintains, if a syndrome of psychical and parapsychical disturbances manifests a demonic presence by its general character, especially by an aversion to sacred things.[41]

However, as Maquart points out, quoting Joseph de Tonquédec, "The hysterical person who takes himself for an instrument of Satan shows a horror for all religious things, an inclination to evil, to gross speech, licentious attitudes, violent agitation, and so on." [42] It is difficult to see how Balducci's interpretation differs from the traditional one in the last analysis. Either the actions of a deranged person can be explained by known natural causes

[39] Citing Frederic W. H. Myers, *Human Personality and Its Survival of Bodily Death* (London 1903) II 201.
[40] A. Huxley, *The Devils of Loudun* (New York 1952) 178.
[41] C. Balducci, *Gli indemonati* (Rome 1959) 324-25. 393-425.
[42] Cf. J. de Tonquédec, *Les maladies nerveuses ou mentales et les manifestations diaboliques* (Paris 1938) 82, cited by Maquart, "Exorcism" 192.

or they cannot, and if they cannot, then some other explanation must be sought.

Before we go further, we may point out here that the tendency to deceive and be deceived is very strong in such cases. Lhermitte has described "how supervision over a possessed person can be cleverly evaded by a hysterical patient," and he adds: "All neurologists know that one must attribute to this neurosis only what one observes directly at first hand, and not all of that!" [43]

Fortunately, in this modern age it is no longer necessary to rely solely upon the testimony of observers. Scientific methods of investigation and recording are available; it is to be hoped that any further claims for genuine demonic possession will be corroborated by this kind of evidence. All past accounts of demonic wonders in cases of alleged possession are suspect to some degree, and some much more so than others. It is therefore disconcerting and discouraging to see many of the more implausible hagiographical tales of possession taken seriously by Rodewyk.[44]

If for the sake of discussion we should grant that such preternatural or naturally mystifying phenomena do occur, what are we to conclude? Aldous Huxley has delivered a rather benign judgment upon the theory of demonic possession:

> There is nothing, so far as I can see, self-contradictory in the idea of possession. The notion is not one to be ruled out *a priori,* on the ground that it is "a relic of ancient superstition." It should be treated rather as a working hypothesis, which may be cautiously entertained in any case where other forms of explanation are found to be inadequate to the facts. In practice modern exorcists seem to be agreed that most cases of suspected possession are in fact due to hysteria and can best be treated by the standard methods of psychiatry. In a few instances, however, they find evidence of something more than hysteria and assert that only exorcism and the casting out of the possessing spirit can effect a cure.[45]

[43] Lhermitte, *Diabolical Possession* 72 n. 16.
[44] Rodewyk's credulity in accepting legendary material is criticized by W. Nastainczyk, *Trierer theologische Zeitschrift* 73 (1964) 124-25.
[45] Huxley, *Devils* 172.

It is true that there is nothing self-contradictory in the concept of possession, but this does not automatically qualify it as a likely explanation, or as a serious working hypothesis. In the first place the notion that certain deranged persons are possessed by a spirit is an extremely crude medical theory widespread among primitive peoples. The concept itself, therefore, had no need of a divine revelation. The fact that Jesus is shown to perform some of his cures in a manner suggesting that he confirmed the popular diagnosis of possession does not mean that he was actually giving divine sanction to the theory, any more than he could be said to underwrite other medical judgments that appear in the gospels, as, for example, when people are said to be "lunatic," that is, moonstruck (Mt. 4, 24; 17, 15).

We saw that in the synoptic tradition all diseases were thought to be under the control of the devil. This notion today receives little support even among those who believe that the bible requires belief in the existence of the devil. It would, therefore, seem possible for them to deny the existence of possessing demons while leaving the existence of the devil intact.

However, the modern advocates of the reality of possession, who are for the most part Roman Catholic theologians, have added to the simple character of the unclean spirits of the gospel (who pass through waterless places seeking for rest when they go out of men's bodies: Mt. 12, 43) concepts evolved out of obsolete and, for the most part, abandoned mythologies and philosophies, which transformed them into fallen angels and pure spirits. The resulting hypothesis of possession, therefore, has very little connection either with scripture or with the observable world, and its claim to be taken seriously must be received with skepticism.

In reviewing Rodewyk's book, J. Sudbrack, a German Jesuit like Rodewyk, objects to any specific case of derangement being classified as diabolical possession on the grounds of unusual symptoms. Though he is traditional enough to assert that there is a devil who is always active in his war of hate against mankind, he believes that a specific crystallization of Satan's direct causality is almost impossible to recognize. He notes that even Catholic scholars are beginning to interpret the gospel possession stories in terms of contemporary cultural influences and mind-sets rather than as literally involving demons. Finally, he insists that even in cases where phenomena are not explainable by present-day science, and where Rodewyk believes that unequivocally sound criteria of the diabolical are present, a scientific attitude urges caution and doubt.[46]

In reporting Rodewyk's current lectures on the subject of possession and exorcism, *Der Spiegel* noted the opposition that he has met in his own order (his situation, we may observe, is the reverse of Friedrich von Spee's), and cited the contrasting views of Rodewyk and Karl Rahner in their sections of the article on possession ("Bessenheit") in the *Lexikon für Theologie und Kirche*.[47] In fact, however, Rahner's views seem closer to Rodewyk's than to Sudbrack's. He agrees with Sudbrack that all the natural evils of this life are influenced by diabolic powers. But he says, or appears to say, that at times genuine cases of possession can be diagnosed as such:

> From the religious point of view, it is neither possible nor particularly desirable to draw a *sharp* distinction between possession and natural sickness, especially as the latter may be a symptom as well as an occasion of possession. . . . Even where a phenomenon is to be deemed possession in the stricter sense, it will be the manifestation of that fundamental diabolical dominion that becomes tangible for us only through the circumstances "permitted" precisely in this case; but which also merely reveals what is always present in the world and therefore does not eliminate natural causes but uses them for its own purposes. To distinguish adequately between diabolical influence on the one hand and the intellectual and imaginative world of a person or a period, dispositions, possible illnesses, even parapsychological faculties on the other, is neither necessary nor possible.[48]

---

[46] J. Sudbrack, *Geist und Leben* 38 (1965) 318-19.

[47] *Der Spiegel* 19,26 (9 June 1965) 51-52.

[48] "Possession," in K. Rahner and H. Vorgrimler, *Theological Dictionary* (ed. C. Ernst, tr. R. Strachan, New York 1965) 365. (I have assumed that this article is by Rahner and not Vorgrimler because of its similarity to Rahner's *Lexikon* article.)

Rahner does not specify the grounds on which it would be possible to define a phenomenon as possession in the stricter sense. But since he assumes not only that genuine possession does exist but also that it sometimes accompanies natural sickness, he must have in mind the sort of specifically diabolical preternatural manifestations that Rodewyk speaks of, or else his position is meaningless. Elsewhere Rahner suggests the manifestations of diabolical possession as a source of a natural demonology independent of divine revelation.[49]

6. Exorcism and Its Effects

In one of the articles on possession just cited Rahner says: "There is no radical dilemma between combating the phenomenon by exorcism (a solemn prayer to God in the name and by the commission of Christ and the Church for his protection against malign powers) and doing so by medicine, especially as every Christian should *pray* for health even in the most 'natural' sickness." [50] He would perhaps be justified in the view that patients can be treated simultaneously by exorcism and medicine if exorcism were only a prayer quietly offered on behalf of those thought to be possessed (although, to force Rahner's view to its logical conclusion, all human adversities should be attacked with exorcisms). However, exorcism is rather a theatrical ritual in which demons as well as God are addressed and which, as has been frequently emphasized by many authors, can of itself induce a state of possession (in the pathological sense). De Tonquédec says: "Exorcism is an impressive ceremony, capable of acting effectively on a sick man's subconsciousness. The adjurations addressed to the demon, the sprinklings with holy water, the stole passed round the patient's neck, the repeated signs of the cross and so forth, can easily call up a diabolical mythomania in word and deed in a psyche already weak. Call the devil and you'll see him; or rather not him, but a portrait made up of the sick man's ideas of him." [51]

[49] K. Rahner "Dämonologie," LTK 3, 145.
[50] Rahner, *Theol. Dict.* 365.
[51] J. de Tonquédec, *Maladies nerveuses,* in Maquart, "Exorcism" 178-79.

De Tonquédec had firsthand familiarity with the effects that could result from using exorcism upon persons who were ill, for he confesses that he himself made this mistake in his early days as official exorcist for the archdiocese of Paris.[52] In the nearly half-century that he held that office he was never convinced that he had come upon a genuine case of possession.

Oesterreich observes that "by artificial means and in appropriate suggestive and autosuggestive conditions it is possible to induce division of the psychic life. Naturally this method might still be applied with success to many ignorant persons, and we should then be in an ideal position, theoretically speaking, to explore the psychology of possession in a truly experimental manner. But from the practical point of view the student could hardly bring himself to provoke these disturbances voluntarily, for, as the literature of the subject shows, they are far easier to cause than to cure." He cites at length a case "in which timely psychiatric treatment intervened before the demoniac visions resulting from a priest's suggestion of the idea of possession had produced derangements of the personality." [53]

However, Oesterreich goes on to say:

As regards the artificial extinction of possession, it has always been suggestive in character and has even resulted from "exorcism," that is to say, the emphatic ordering of the so-called demon to leave the possessed person. The stories of the gospels are in this respect typical of the procedure of exorcism at all times. It has never varied, either in the time of Jesus or during the millenaries before and since. . . .

Exorcism presents the exact counterpart of the genesis of possession. In the same way that the latter springs from a man's belief that he is possessed, conversely it disappears, when the exorcism is successful, through his belief that it will no longer continue.[54]

From this point of view one could perhaps make a case for the ad-

[52] De Tonquédec, *op. cit.* 204.
[53] Oesterreich, *Possession* 98-99.
[54] *Ibid.* 100.

visability of using exorcism as a cure in a situation where the symptoms of possession (or pseudo-possession) are already well advanced, whether or not the exorcist has been able to satisfy the demands of the *Roman Ritual* in making certain of the demonic nature of the affliction.

However, Sudbrack intimates in his review of Rodewyk's book that the practice of exorcism has in the past caused many medical precautions and treatments to be neglected. Klaus Ernst points out that, in the days when persons whose symptoms would now suggest schizophrenia were thought to be possessed by a devil, the exorcist tried to drive out the demonic personality, whereas modern psychotherapy aims at the integration of the various elements in the patient's consciousness.[55] Lhermitte reports that many of the pseudo-demoniacs that have been brought to his attention have eventually lapsed into schizophrenia.[56] This kind of deterioration is to be feared from exorcistic practices or any other encouragement of the concept of possession in the minds of deranged persons.

Until, therefore, the theory of demonic possession can make a more respectable case for itself, the exorcist seems as much out of place in a sickroom or mental asylum as a witchdoctor. For while the latter could no doubt effect the same kind of cures on patients of certain conditioned mentalities as exorcists have done in the past, a safer and more enlightened method would be to attempt to disabuse the victims of their fixations of possession by normal therapeutic methods.

[55] K. Ernst, "Zeitbedingtes und Zeitloses in der Behandlung seelisch Kranker; über sieben Protokolle von Exorzismen bei schizophrenieähnlichen Hysterien im 16. Jahrhundert," *Neue zürcher Zeitung* (Foreign ed. no. 29, Sat., 30 Jan. 1965) fol. 21, esp. 21v col. 2.
[56] Lhermitte, *Diabolical Possession* 88.

V
DEMONIC TEMPTATION

Later theologians have often assumed that the devil and his demons persecute mankind in two radically different ways. One of these ways, demonic possession and the corporal affliction of individuals, is assumed to make extraordinary demands upon a demon's resources, apart from the fact that it is only very rarely permitted by God. The other way, temptation, is, we are assured, the demons' ordinary mode of operation; here they are supposedly able to function with a great deal of freedom. It is on this premise that F. X. Maquart, for instance, bases his study of possession and exorcism in the essay cited in the last chapter. He believes that possession is preternatural—that it involves diabolical marvels—whereas temptation can be caused by the evil spirits without resorting to the miraculous.[1]

This distinction, however, has little or no basis in patristic or scholastic theology. Specifically, as we shall see, it is not found in the writings of St. Thomas Aquinas, upon whom Maquart professes to rely philosophically and theologically.

The distinction may have originated partially as a result of the Protestant reevaluation of the function of evil spirits. We saw that Reginald Scot completely denied the ability of evil spirits to act upon the bodies of men, since it would be a kind of miracle surpassing the capabilities of the spiritual nature of demons. He did, however, admit that they could act upon men spiritually by the invisible and imperceptible communication of evil suggestions, in the way, for instance, that Satan tempted Eve by "creeping into her consciousness."

[1] Maquart, "Exorcism and Diabolical Manifestation" 178.

1. Early Theories

The New Testament also provides a very clear distinction between possession and temptation, since, as we have had occasion to emphasize before, the demons or unclean spirits that possess men's bodies in the gospels do not operate as tempters; the latter function is reserved for the devil himself, who took this characteristic directly from the satan of the Old Testament, in the book of Job and first book of Chronicles. When he emerges as the anti-messianic ruler of the world in the gospels and is portrayed as coming to tempt Christ, he is specifically designated as "the Tempter" (Mt. 4, 3).

The temptation of Christ, we saw, follows the standard Jewish literary pattern of the just man who remains faithful to his divine mission in the face of temptation. For the purposes of dramatization the devil seemingly appears in visible form—the only time he does so in the New Testament. In the more historical episodes, as we pointed out, Christ is directly tempted or thwarted by human adversaries and not by the devil. But occasionally the influence of the devil is suggested. A particularly striking example occurs in the narrative of the Last Supper, when Satan is said to put the idea of betraying Jesus into Judas' heart (Jn. 13, 2).

Once the devil and the demons had been united in patristic thought in terms of mythical fallen angels, the distinction between the demons as possessing spirits and the devil as tempter was no longer clear. The Jewish-Christian theory of vice-demons added a moral dimension to the disturbances caused by the unclean spirits of the gospels; and Origen specifically stated that the passions caused by the demons in charge of the various vices could result in madness, that is, in demonic possession in the fullest corporal sense (*De princ.* 3,2,2). Furthermore Origen adopted the Qumran theme of the two angels as used by the Jewish-Christian *Shepherd* of Hermas, according to which each individual is attended by two angels: "whenever good thoughts arise in our hearts, they are suggested by the good angel; but when of a contrary kind, they are the instigation of the evil angel" (*ibid.* 3,2,4). This tradition of a "guardian demon" for each man lived on for centuries after, and is found, for example, in Peter Lombard in the Middle Ages and Francis Suarez in the Renaissance.[2]

In *The Life of St. Antony,* ascribed to Athanasius, Bishop of Alexandria, and written in the middle of the fourth century, we have a good example of the mental campaign against virtue thought to be waged, if not by a permanently assigned demon, at least by the devil himself, who seems to be omnipresent and able to take advantage of every opportunity for evil simultaneously all over the world.

As a youth, we read, Antony began an ascetical life:

> But the devil, the hater and envier of good, could not bear to see such resolution in a young man, but set about employing his customary tactics also against him. First, he tried to make him desert the ascetic life by putting him in mind of his property, the care of his sister, the attachments of kindred, the love of money, the love of fame, the myriad pleasures of eating, and all the other amenities of life. Finally, he represented to him the austerity and all the toil that go with virtue, suggesting that the body is weak and time is long. In short, he raised in his mind a great dust cloud of arguments, intending to make him abandon his set purpose.
>
> The enemy saw, however, that he was powerless in the face of Antony's determination and that it was rather he who was being bested because of the man's steadfastness and vanquished by his solid faith and routed by Antony's constant prayer. He then put his trust in the weapons that are *in the navel of his own belly* (Job. 40, 16). Priding himself in these —for they are his choice snare against the young—he advanced to attack the young man, troubling him so by night and harassing him by day, that even those who saw Antony could perceive the struggle going on between the two. The enemy would suggest filthy thoughts, but the other would dissipate them by his prayers; he would try to incite him to lust, but Antony, sensing shame, would gird his body with his faith, with his prayers and his fasting. The wretched devil

[2] See Sebastian Weber, *De singulorum hominum daemone impugnatore* (Rome 1938).

even dared to masquerade as a woman by night and to im-
personate such in every possible way, merely in order to deceive Antony. But he filled his thoughts with Christ and
reflected upon the nobility of the soul that comes from him,
and its spirituality, and thus quenched the glowing coal of
temptation. And again the enemy suggested pleasure's seduc-
tive charm. But Antony, angered, of course, and grieved, kept
his thoughts upon the threat of fire and the pain of the worm.
Holding these up as his shield, he came through unscathed.
(c. 5)[3]

Because of Antony's resounding victory over evil early in his
ascetic career, the devil was forced to abandon his campaign of internal suggestion:

Finally when the dragon could not conquer Antony by this
last means either, but saw himself thrust out of his heart,
gnashing his teeth, as scripture says, he changed his person, so
to speak. As he is in his heart, precisely so did he appear to
him—as a black boy; and as though cringing to him, he no
longer assailed him with thoughts—for he had been ousted,
the imposter—but now using a human voice, he said: "Many
a man have I deceived and very many have I overthrown;
but now when I attacked you and your efforts as I have done
with many others, I proved too weak." (c. 6)

In time, however, the devil began a series of external assaults
against the saint. First "he came one night with a great number of
demons and lashed him so unmercifully that he lay on the ground
speechless from the pain" (c. 8). But when he recovered he re-
turned to his regular practices. Enraged at this, the devil called together his demons and said: "You see that we have not stopped
this fellow, neither by the spirit of fornication nor by blows; on the
contrary, he even challenges us. Let us go after him in another
way." The "other way" is the form of attack that generations of
painters have singled out as *the* temptation of St. Antony:

[3] Athanasius, *The Life of Saint Antony* (tr. R. T. Meyer, Ancient Christian
Writers 10, Westminster 1950) 22-23.

That night, therefore, they made such a din that the whole place seemed to be shaken by an earthquake. It was as though demons were breaking through the four walls of the little chamber and bursting through them in the forms of beasts and reptiles. All at once the place was filled with the phantoms of lions, bears, leopards, bulls, and of serpents, asps, and scorpions, and of wolves; and each moved according to the shape it had assumed. The lion roared, ready to spring upon him, the bull appeared about to gore him through, the serpent writhed without quite reaching him, the wolf was rushing straight at him; and the noises emitted simultaneously by all the apparitions were frightful and the fury shown was fierce.

Antony, pummeled and goaded by them, felt even severer pain in his body; yet he lay there fearless and all the more alert in spirit. He groaned, it is true, because of the pain that racked his body, but his mind was master of the situation, and, as if to mock them, he said: "If you had any power in you, it would have been enough for just one of you to come; but the Lord has taken your strength away, and so you are trying, if possible, to scare me out of my wits by your numbers. It is a sign of your helplessness that you ape the forms of brutes." (c. 9)

Among the many other startling occurrences that befell Antony during his long life in the Egyptian desert, there is one in which he was summoned to the door of his abode:

He rose and saw a monster resembling a man as far as the thighs, but having legs and feet like an ass. Antony simply made the sign of the cross and said: "I am Christ's servant. If you are on a mission against me, here I am." But the monster with its demons fled so fast that its speed caused it to fall and die. And the death of the monster stood for the fall of the demons: they were making every effort to drive him back from the desert, and they could not. (c. 53)

This passage reminds us of the transformation that Isaiah's desert creatures underwent at the hands of the Egyptian translators of the

Septuagint, where demons and ass-centaurs meet together in the wilderness (Is. 34, 14). We have seen the great influence that Egyptian demonology had upon the development of Christian demon-lore, both from the Septuagint and from the philosophies and religions (like Valentinian gnosticism) that left their mark on the liturgy and on thinkers like Origen. The enormous popularity of *The Life of St. Antony* resulted in another massive infusion of demonological fantasies from Egypt into the Christian world at large. The movement was continued with great enthusiasm in the accounts of the conferences of the desert abbots that John Cassian imported to Gaul at the end of the fourth century.

Johannes Quasten points out that Antony "regards monastic life as a martyrdom and the monk as the successor to the martyr. Just as the martyr was thought to fight with Satan in his suffering, so the monk was supposed to wage a continuous battle against the demons." [4]

Much of the persecution of the early Christians was carried out in the name of the pagan religion, and the identification of the pagan gods with the demons of Christianity resulted in the idea that the persecution was directly sponsored by the devil and his minions. The demands of the pagan rituals and priests were, therefore, another source of demonic temptations and errors that Christians had to resist. It was, so the ecclesiastical authorities believed, especially in the realm of divination that the aid of evil powers was sought, and the Christian apologists were at pains to discredit their ability to foretell the future. The practitioners of divination were, of course, like the magicians, unaware of the diabolical nature of their art until the Christians pointed it out to them. Origen, for instance, admitted that some kind of valid prognostication could be obtained from observing birds of augury. But he believed that the birds and other such animals were demonically possessed for the purpose of tempting men:

In my opinion, however, it is certain wicked demons, and, so to speak, of the race of Titans or Giants, who have been guilty of impiety towards the true God, and towards the angels in

[4] J. Quasten, *Patrology* III (1960) 41-42.

heaven, and who have fallen from it, and who haunt the denser parts of bodies, and frequent unclean places upon earth, and who, possessing some power of distinguishing future events, because they are without bodies of earthly material, engage in an employment of this kind, and desiring to lead the human race away from the true God, secretly enter the bodies of the more rapacious and savage and wicked of animals, and stir them up to do whatever they choose; or they turn the fancies of these animals to make flights and movements of various kinds, in order that men may be caught by the divining power that is in the irrational animals, and neglect to seek after the God who contains all things, or to search after the pure worship of God, but allow their reasoning powers to grovel on the earth, and amongst birds and serpents, and even foxes and wolves. (*Against Celsus* 4,92)

According to St. Antony, in the speech that Athanasius gives him, when the demons are unable to overpower their victims by suggesting evil thoughts or appearing in fearful shapes "they advance once more with new strategy. They pretend to prophesy and to foretell future events. They show themselves taller than the roof and burly and bulky. Their purpose is, if possible, to snatch off by such phantoms those whom they could not deceive with thoughts" (c. 23). He later explains the fraud that is involved in the prophecy of demons. He admits that they can often accurately predict various events, such as the arrival of visitors in a city. But, he asks, "what is wonderful about that, if they who have lighter bodies than men, seeing that men have set out on a journey, outdistance them and announce their arrival? . . . Often, though, travelers turn back and their report is false." (c. 31)

St. Augustine in his work on the *Divination of Demons* makes the same point. Because of the demons' aerial bodies and the swift mobility and sharpness of perception that such bodies permit, they can know many things long before they come to the attention of the human senses. But they are not to be held in honor for such abilities, he says, since even many animals have more refined senses than humans (c. 3).

2. The Theory of Internal Demonic Temptation

The two Egyptian writers we have quoted, Origen and Athanasius, ascribed to demons the power of suggesting evil thoughts to the minds of men. Augustine, likewise a North African, also believed that demons had this ability. For example, early in the fifth century at Hippo, in a sermon on John 13, 2 ("the devil had already put it into the heart of Judas Iscariot, Simon's son, to betray him"), he said:

Such a putting into the heart is a spiritual suggestion, and enters not by the ear but through the thoughts, and thereby not in a way that is corporal, but spiritual. . . . But how such things are done, as that devilish suggestions should be introduced, and so mingle with human thoughts that a man accounts them his own, how can he know? Nor can we doubt that good suggestions are likewise made by a good spirit in the same unobservable and spiritual way; but it is a matter of concern to which of these the human mind yields assent, either as deservedly left without, or graciously aided by, the divine assistance. (Tractate 55, 4 NPNF)

A quarter of a century earlier Augustine attempted to explain how demons could make their evil suggestions. In reply to the question of Nebridius, he says:

It is my opinion that every movement of the mind affects in some degree the body. We know that this is patent even to our senses, dull and sluggish though they are, when the movements of the mind are somewhat vehement, as when we are angry, or sad, or joyful. Whence we may conjecture that, in like manner, when thought is busy, although no bodily effect of the mental act is discernible by us, there may be some such effect discernible by beings of aerial or ethereal essence whose perceptive faculty is in the highest degree acute—so much so, that, in comparison with it, our faculties are scarcely worthy to be called perceptive. Therefore these footprints of its motion, so to speak, which the mind impresses on the body, may perchance not only remain, but remain as it were with the force of a habit; and it may be that, when these are secretly stirred and played upon, they bear thoughts and dreams into our minds, according to the pleasure of the person moving or touching them; and this is done with marvelous facility. For if, as is manifest, the attainments of our earthborn and sluggish bodies in the department of exercise, for example, in the playing of musical instruments, dancing on the tightrope, and so forth, are almost incredible, it is by no means unreasonable to suppose that beings which act with the powers of an aerial or ethereal body upon our bodies, and are by the constitution of their natures able to pass unhindered through these bodies, should be capable of much greater quickness in moving whatever they wish, while we, though not perceiving what they do, are nevertheless affected by the results of their activity. We have a somewhat parallel instance in the fact that we do not perceive how it is that superfluity of bile impels us to more frequent outbursts of passionate feeling; and yet it does produce this effect, while this superfluity of bile is itself an effect of our yielding to such passionate feelings. (Letter 9.3 NPNF)

When Peter Lombard in the twelfth century takes up the problem of the nature and abilities of angels and demons, he does not decide the question whether, as Augustine seemed to hold, angels have bodies, or whether they are incorporeal. He goes on to ask if demons, with or without some kind of body of their own, can enter completely into the bodies of men and penetrate into their souls, or if, on the contrary, they are only said to enter men because of the evil effects they cause by inflicting various kinds of harassment and temptations upon them with God's permission. He quotes from Augustine (or rather from a writing mistakenly attributed to Augustine) the following opinion: "We do not believe that the demons can so operate that they enter into the soul with their whole being, but rather they join themselves to it by contact and forceful pressure; the mind can be entered only by him who created it, who is by nature incorporeal and able to plumb the depths of what he has made." [5] Lombard also quotes the Venerable Bede to the effect

[5] Pseudo-Augustine, *De ecclesiasticis dogmatibus* 50 (PL 42, 1221).

that demons cannot enter the hearts of men. Bede is commenting on the question of Peter to Ananias, "Why has Satan filled your heart?" (Acts 5, 3), and says:

> No creature can fill the soul and mind of man with its being except the Trinity who created him. For it is only by the operation and impulse of the will that the mind can be filled with created things. Now Satan fills the mind of a man and the depths of his heart, not by entering into him and his senses and, so to speak, going in through the gate of his heart, since this power belongs to God alone; but he enters like a crafty, wicked, fallacious, and fraudulent deceiver, by drawing the human soul to those dispositions that he is filled with, by means of thoughts and incentives to vice. Therefore Satan filled the heart of Ananias not by entering it himself but by implanting the poison of his wickedness.[6]

Lombard concludes that "these authorities show that demons do not enter the hearts of men in their own persons, but only by the effect of their wickedness; and they are said to be expelled from them when they are not allowed to do any harm." [7]

By the middle of the next century the theory that angels are bodiless had won the theological field for all practical purposes. The analysis of St. Thomas Aquinas was particularly influential and remains so to this day. Through a series of philosophical observations on what he conceived to be the actual nature of the cosmos, Thomas became convinced of the existence of beings completely free of any material element or component, so that the ladder of being might be complete and the world be the work of perfection to be expected of an omnipotent creator.[8] He identified these pure spirits with the angels and demons of Christian tradition.

In Thomas' view, angels possessed intellects vastly superior to man's; he believed that their basic mental abilities remained unchanged in those angels who fell from grace and became demons.

---

[6] Bede, *Commentary on Acts* 5 (PL 92, 954).
[7] Lombard, *Sentences* 2, 8 (PL 192, 667-69).
[8] See, for example, *Summa theologiae* 1, 50, 1 and *De spiritualibus creaturis* 5.

St. Augustine, on the other hand, was closer to the hagiographical tradition of the dull-witted and easily defeated demon. He admitted, as we have seen, their superiority to men in the acuteness of their senses and the advantages of invisibility and swiftness, and he also conceded that they had a longer period of experience to draw upon; but he did not regard them as superior to men in reason.

However, a number of considerations tended to equalize the practical abilities of the demons in the systems of Augustine and Thomas. In the first place, all Christian writers emphasize that the evil spirits can do nothing against man without permission of God, who never allows temptation to exceed a person's powers of resistance. Furthermore, Thomas holds that fallen spirits are not given full access to the spiritual faculties (that is, the intellect and will) of men, but must infer their thoughts and desires from physical indications (*Evil* 16, 8). [9] This position agrees with Augustine's early view as expressed in the *Divination,* where he says that "demons at times become thoroughly aware of men's dispositions with the greatest ease, not only from what the men say, but also from what they conceive in their thoughts, when signs of what is going on in the mind appear in the body." [10] But Augustine had second thoughts on the subject when he wrote his *Retractations* or revisions of his earlier works. He says of this passage: "I spoke of a very obscure matter more positively and boldly than I should have. True, it is known even by various kinds of actual experience that these things do come to the knowledge of demons. But whether certain signs are present in the body of what men are thinking, which are discernible by them but hidden from us, or whether they have their knowledge by another way, and that a spiritual one, is a matter that men can ascertain only with great difficulty or not at all." [11]

We remember Augustine speculating that the physical traces of mental activity in a man could be so moved by demons as to have thoughts and dreams introduced into the mind (*Letter* 9, 3). Even in the opinion of Bede that Lombard adopted, the devil can com-

---

[9] Thomas' views on the evil spirits are most fully expounded in this *quaestio disputata* or series of graduate seminars on the nature of evil (*De malo*).

[10] *Augustine, Divination of Demons* 5 (CSEL 41, 608; PL 40, 586).

[11] Augustine, *Retractations* 2, 56 (CSEL 36, 167, PL 32, 643).

municate thoughts to a person's mind, although he is denied actual entry to it. But in the thirteenth century Lombard's commentators refined the notion that God alone could have access to the human intellect and will, and they now maintained that demons could hold no spiritual communication with men or infuse thoughts directly into their minds, but were restricted to the material or sensitive part of the human person. This was the view of St. Bonaventure and the other Franciscan disciples of Alexander of Hales, and of St. Thomas himself.[12]

The manner in which a demonic temptation occurred under this restriction was similar to that suggested by Augustine in his letter to Nebridius, but it was analyzed in terms of medieval psychology. Thomas follows Augustine in believing that demons operate by moving material things or the "seeds" of things from place to place. Accordingly, when tempting men they manipulate the spirits and humors, that is, the internal bodily fluids, in order to activate the sense appetite, which in turn summons up images stored in the memory. By reviving appropriate images in this way, or by arranging new combinations from various single images, the demons manage to present the mind with provocations to indulge in sinful thoughts and desires (*Evil* 16, 10-12). Besides tampering with the imagination, demons can also interfere with external sensation by their movement of bodily fluids and can arouse the emotions to anger, lust, or other vicious passions (*Evil* 3, 4). We saw earlier that, in Thomas' view, demons can interfere with the sense appetite in order to prevent sexual arousal, and thereby cause impotence, and that this is regularly done by those evil spirits who are in league with witches.

The theologians' scruple that denied the demons direct access to the human mind on the grounds that it is God alone "who searches the reins and the heart" (Rev. 2, 23) has often had no effect upon authors of spiritual treatises, who normally seem to envisage diabolical temptation as a kind of spiritual whispering, a direct communication of thoughts to the mind. This point of view was explicitly expressed by the seventeenth-century Anglican clergyman Robert

---

[12] *Summa fratris Alexandri* 2, 40, 2.4 (Quaracchi ed. II 259-62); Bonaventure, *Commentary on the Sentences* 2, 8, 2, 1, 3; Thomas, *Comm. Sent.* 2, 8, 1, 5.

Burton, who says in his *Anatomy of Melancholy*: "Many think that [the devil] can work upon the body, but not upon the mind. But experience pronounceth otherwise, that he can work both upon body and mind. . . . For being a spiritual body, he struggles with our spirits, saith Rogers, and suggests, according to Cardan, *verba sine voce, species sine visu,* envy, lust, anger, and so on, as he sees men inclined." [13] A modern example of this view of the temptations of evil spirits is found in the work of another Anglican writer on Christian spirituality, the late C. S. Lewis, whose humorous account of diabolical machinations in the *Screwtape Letters* reflects an attitude that he and many of his contemporaries, especially among Roman Catholic theologians, have taken seriously.

In Thomas' view both bodily affliction and temptation are accomplished by the same demonic technique: the manipulation of matter in space. We recall that Origen had taught that the passions caused by the demons in charge of various vices could sometimes dominate men so intensely that they would go mad, and the demons would take possession of their entire sensitive nature (*De princ.* 3,2,2). Similarly, Thomas notes that the demons act on the bodily fluids rather than directly on the various organs of the man they are tempting because such direct action would result in pain (and, we may add, defeat their purpose of summoning up provocative memories and fantasies). Although this demonic activity can result in depriving a person of his reason, as in the possessed (*arreptitii*), God does not always permit it (*Evil* 16, 11 ad 9-10).

While, therefore, he apparently believes that God more often permits temptation than possession, he does not believe that possession is produced by a method more unusual or marvelous than the method of temptation. Possession does, however, imply a more continuous demonic presence than temptation. In another place, in answer to the question whether the devil actually inhabits a person in the state of mortal sin, he says that only God can inhabit the soul or mind; since the devil's suggestions are external to it he inhabits it only by his effects. However, he goes on, the devil can actually inhabit the body, as is shown in cases of possession (*Quaestiones quodlibetales* 3,3,3). In this Thomas affirms more than Lombard was willing to admit.

[13] R. Burton, *The Anatomy of Melancholy* 1, 2, 1, 2 (London 1849) 128-29.

3. The Discernment of Spirits

In the literature of Christian spirituality there is a long tradition of analyzing the various effects attributed to the spirit world to determine whether they are produced by good or evil spirits. Similar kinds of analyses can be found in the writings of the Essene sect at Qumran with their descriptions of men under the control either of the prince of light or of the prince of darkness. It is no surprise, then, that one of the earliest and clearest expressions of this tradition in Christianity is found in the *Shepherd* of Hermas, which is clearly linked to Essene thought. Hermas receives the following instruction on the subject:

> There are two angels with a man—one of righteousness and the other of iniquity. . . . The angel of righteousness is gentle and modest, meek and peaceful. When, therefore, he ascends into your heart, forthwith he talks to you of righteousness, purity, chastity, contentment, and of every righteous deed and glorious virtue. When all these ascend into your heart, know that the angel of righteousness is with you. These are the deeds of the angel of righteousness. Trust him, then, and his works. Look now at the works of the angel of iniquity. First, he is wrathful and bitter and foolish, and his works are evil and ruin the servants of God. When, then, he ascends into your heart, know him by his works. . . . When anger comes upon you, or harshness, know that he is in you; and you will know this to be the case also when you are attacked by a longing after many transactions and the richest delicacies and drunken revels and divers luxuries and things improper and by a hankering after women and by overreaching and pride and blustering and by whatever is like to these. When these ascend into your heart, know that the angel of iniquity is in you. Now that you know his works, depart from him and in no respect trust him, because his deeds are evil and unprofitable to the servants of God. (39 = Mand. 6, 2 ANF)

This passage suggests that all virtuous thoughts or impulses are produced by or with the aid of a good angel, and on the other hand, no vicious tendency appears without the intervention of an evil spirit. Origen, we recall, cited the first line of this instruction as one of his authorities for the belief that every man was constantly accompanied by an evil as well as a good angel. The rest of the passage, as well as other parts of the *Shepherd,* reflect the Jewish-Christian notion that all sins are connected with demons of vice who dwell in the heart of the sinner. Origen, however, when he cites Hermas, makes it clear that he believes some thoughts come from ourselves and not from either good or evil spirits. He finds it "clearly evident that there are certain transgressions which we by no means commit under the pressure of malignant powers, while there are others, again, to which we are incited by instigation on their part to excessive and immoderate indulgence" (*De princ.* 3,2,3).

Another celebrated set of rules for the discernment of spirits occurs in the speech of Antony in Athanasius' biography. He says that by the help of God the presence of either the good or the evil spirits can easily be distinguished:

A vision of the holy ones is not turbulent, for *he shall not contend, nor cry out, neither shall any man hear his voice* (Mt. 12, 19). But it comes so quietly and gently that instantly joy and gladness and courage arise in the soul. For with them is our Lord who is our joy, and the power of God the Father. And the thoughts of the soul remain untroubled and unruffled, so that in its own bright transparency it is able to behold those who appear. A longing for things divine and for the things of the future life takes possession of it, and its desire is that it may be wholly united to them if it could but depart with them. But if some, being human, are seized with fear at the vision of the good, then those who appear dispel the fear by love, as did Gabriel for Zachary, and the angel who appeared to the women at the holy sepulcher, and the angel who spoke to the shepherds in the gospel: *Fear not.* Fear in these cases is not from cravenness of soul, but from an awareness of the presence of higher beings. Such, then, is the vision of the holy ones.

On the other hand, the attack and appearance of the evil ones is full of confusion, accompanied by crashing, roaring, and shouting; it could well be the tumult produced by rude boys and robbers. This at once begets terror in the soul, disturbance and confusion of thoughts, dejection, hatred of ascetics, indifference, sadness, remembrance of kinsfolk, and fear of death; and then a desire for evil, a disdain for virtue, and a complete subversion of character. When, therefore, you have a vision and are afraid, if then the fear is taken from you immediately and in its place comes ineffable joy and contentment, and courage and recovery of strength and calmness of thought and the other things I have mentioned, and stoutheartedness, too, and love of God, then be of good cheer and pray—for your joy and your soul's tranquillity betoken the holiness of Him who is present. Thus Abraham, seeing the Lord, rejoiced (Jn. 8, 56); and John, hearing the voice of Mary, the mother of God, leaped for joy (Lk. 1, 41). But when you have certain visions, and confusion overtakes you and there is tumult from without and earthly apparitions and threats of death and all the things I have mentioned, then know that the visit is from the wicked. (cc. 35-36)

Even though Antony makes it clear that the first tactic of the devil is the suggestion of tempting thoughts, he gives no rules for recognizing these, but limits himself to categorizing external apparitions and the reactions that they cause in the observer. It is important to note that Antony seems to specify that ease in identifying spirits comes only with the help of God. In doing so he anticipates the school of thought that holds that the discernment of spirits involves the special assistance of God, and is in fact a charism or gift of the Holy Spirit like the power of prophecy.

Of the many subsequent analyses aimed at detecting the devil's influence, perhaps the best known is the one that appears in the *Spiritual Exercises* of Ignatius of Loyola under the title of "Rules for the Discernment of Spirits." However, though these rules speak in terms of the good and evil spirit, they are not aimed at specifying the sources of thoughts and emotions or differentiating those caused by the devil from those inspired by God or those arising from purely natural causes. Ignatius' purpose is rather to discuss the effects of various kinds of emotional and mental states.

Those that have harmful effects he characterizes as belonging to the evil angel, not necessarily because they originate with an evil spirit (though he believes that such can be the case), but because they are in accord with the devil's purposes.

Many of the commentators upon the *Exercises,* however, have misunderstood the rules for discernment and have assumed that they were designed precisely to discover the devil's actual presence.[14] This notion is still widespread, especially among Jesuits, who ordinarily adhere closely to the *Exercises* when conducting spiritual retreats. In following this interpretation they are, like the would-be Thomists described above, closer to the thought of Robert Burton than to that of Ignatius. Burton gives the following criteria for recognizing the devil's temptations:

The devil is still ready to corrupt, trouble, and divert our souls, to suggest such blasphemous thoughts into our fantasies, ungodly, profane, monstrous, and wicked conceits. If they come from Satan, they are more speedy, fearful, and violent, the parties cannot avoid them; they are more frequent, I say, and monstrous when they come; for the devil he is a spirit, and hath means and opportunities to mingle himself with our spirits, and sometimes more slyly, sometimes more abruptly and openly, to suggest such devilish thoughts into our hearts; he insults and domineers in melancholy distempered fantasies and persons especially; melancholy is *balneum diaboli,* as Serapio holds, the devil's bath, and invites him to come to it. As a sick man frets, raves in his fits, speaks and doth he knows not what, the devil violently compels such crazed souls to think such damned thoughts against their wills, they cannot but do it; sometimes more continuate, or by fits, he takes his advantage, as the subject is less able to resist, he aggravates, extenuates, affirms, denies, damns, confounds the spirits, troubles heart, brain, humors, organs, senses, and wholly domineers in their imaginations. If they proceed from themselves, such thoughts, they are remiss and moderate, not so violent and monstrous, not so frequent. The devil commonly suggests

14 See Joseph Pegon, "Discernement des esprits," *Dictionnaire de spiritualité* 3 (1957) 1274.

things opposite to nature, opposite to God and his word, impious, absurd, such as a man would never of himself, or could not, conceive; they strike terror and horror into the parties' own hearts. For if he or they be asked whether they do approve of suchlike thoughts or no, they answer, and their own souls truly dictate as much, they abhor them as hell and the devil himself, they would fain think otherwise if they could; he hath thought otherwise, and with all his soul desires so to think again; he doth resist, and hath some good motions intermixed now and then, so that such blasphemous, impious, unclean thoughts, are not his own, but the devil's; they proceed not from him, but from a crazed fantasy, distempered humors, black fumes which offend his brain; they are thy crosses, the devil's sins, and he shall answer for them; he doth enforce thee to do that which thou dost abhor, and didst never give consent to; and although he hath sometimes so slyly set upon thee, and so far prevailed, as to make thee in some sort to assent to such wicked thoughts, to delight in, yet they have not proceeded from a confirmed will in thee, but are of that nature which thou dost afterwards reject and abhor. Therefore be not overmuch troubled and dismayed with such kind of suggestions, at least if they please thee not, because they are not thy personal sins, for which thou shalt incur the wrath of God or his displeasure; contemn, neglect them, let them go as they come, strive not too violently, or trouble thyself too much, but as our Savior said to Satan in like case, say thou: "Avoid, Satan, I detest thee and them." *Satanae est mala ingerere,* saith Austin, *nostrum non consentire:* as Satan labors to suggest, so must we strive not to give consent, and it will be sufficient. The more anxious and solicitous thou art, the more perplexed, the more thou shalt otherwise be troubled and entangled.[15]

This advice is a good example of how the concept of diabolical temptation is put to use by many spiritual directors even now. As for Burton's method of determining the devil's presence from the unusual strength or perversity of a temptation, the same approach

[15] Burton, *Anatomy of Melancholy* 3, 4, 2, 6 (729-30).

can be found in a recent work of a Benedictine psychologist, Willibald Demal, who says:

> The plague of temptation (*obsessio*) consists in the influence of the devil on the external or internal senses. It is known that the devil attempts to lead the saints astray through temptations of the senses of vision, hearing, and feeling. Similarly he can influence the internal senses, imagination, and memory, as well as the passions. Such temptations may be readily distinguished from usual tribulations by their longer duration and greater intensity. First, the priest will employ the same remedies as in the case of normal temptations. But should there be at least a moral probability for the existence of *obsessio,* he will also privately and secretly use exorcism.[16]

Demal fails to indicate how diabolical temptations differ from the morbid or neurotic compulsions and fixations that he discusses later in his book.[17] Jean Lhermitte has described the various pathological reactions that can occur when a sick person is convinced of the incursions of the devil. In addition to the ordinary forms of pseudo-possession that we saw him describe in the last chapter, there is the phenomenon that he terms "demonopathic delirium," based on the division of personality found in the more common kinds of persecution mania. "Do we not find in these patients," he says, "all the signs of an invasion by a personality alien to their ego—a personality which reveals itself by compulsions, forced actions, inhibitions, by sounds heard perfectly clearly, distinctly, and frequently, by numerous sensory and psychic hallucinations, and by ineffable sensations of an influence present within or around them: The essence of this influence remains a mystery until the day when the patient becomes convinced, during one of these attacks of delirium, that it is indeed an evil spirit who directs his actions, induces his feelings and ideas, in fact who possesses him and holds him at his mercy." [18]

[16] W. Demal, *Pastoral Psychology in Practice* (tr. J. W. Conway, New York 1955) 46-47.
[17] *Ibid.* 218-21.
[18] J. Lhermitte, "Pseudo-Possession," *Satan* (New York 1952) 297-98.

If the experiences that Lhermitte details here are not a sufficient indication of the presence of the devil, it is obvious that the criteria that Burton and Demal propose have no validity whatever. There is, in fact, a long tradition in Christianity paralleling that of the discernment of spirits which denies the possibility of distinguishing diabolical temptations from natural ones, simply on the grounds that evil spirits are able to simulate natural thoughts and emotions.

Origen says, "With respect to the thoughts which proceed from our heart, or the recollection of things which we have done, or the contemplation of any things or causes whatever, we find that they sometimes proceed from ourselves, and sometimes are originated by the opposing powers; not seldom also are they suggested by God, or by the holy angels. Now such a statement will perhaps appear incredible, unless it be confirmed by the testimony of holy scripture" (*De princ*. 3,2,4,). He goes on to prove from sacred writings not only that thoughts come from the outside, but also that they arise within ourselves. The implication is that it is impossible to identify the source of thoughts without a divine revelation.

This implication is made explicit in Augustine. We recall that he said, in commenting on John's gospel, that devilish suggestions can be introduced and so mingled with human thoughts "that a man accounts them his own" (55, 4). Elsewhere he says: "Discretion is very difficult when the evil spirit acts in a relatively tranquil fashion, and without any disturbance of the body applies himself to the human spirit and says whatever he can, and also when he speaks the truth and urges what is useful, transfiguring himself as an angel of light, as it is written (2 Cor. 11, 14), in order that, gaining trust in himself in what is obviously good, he may seduce one to his own purposes." [19] He goes on to say that he does not think discernment possible in such cases without the gift of God of which the apostle spoke (1 Cor. 12, 10). Augustine's analysis accords with that of Thomas, who, as we saw, described how the evil spirits could call up tempting images in the mind without causing any kind of pain or unusual disturbance. Robert Burton believed that we know the internal temptations of the devil by experience. Thomas, however, does not appeal to experience but to reason. He assumes that a great

[19] Augustine, *De genesi ad literam* 12, 13 (CSEL 28, 398).

many sins are committed at the instigation of the devil, far more than could be accounted for by his external apparitions; he concludes therefore that he also tempts invisibly and internally (*Evil* 3, 4).

In *The Imitation of Christ,* the fifteenth-century devotional treatise traditionally ascribed to Thomas à Kempis, we are told: "It is difficult to be certain whether it is a good spirit or a bad one that prompts one to this or that, and even to know whether you are being moved by your own spirit." [20] Demal himself admits, "We are well advised to consider as diabolical phenomena only those that can be so identified on the ground of their extraordinary nature or the totality of conditions and circumstances." [21] But this is precisely the same rule that the *Roman Ritual* insists upon to determine the presence of an evil spirit in a suspected victim of possession. If, then, the methods for discovering genuine cases of possession are highly unsatisfactory, they could hardly be less so when applied to determine an alien spiritual influence behind troublesome thoughts or emotions. If Demal adhered rigorously to his rule, he would never be able to determine the presence of diabolical temptation. However, his advice for dealing with such temptation makes a strict observation of his cautionary rule less necessary than in suspected cases of possession. Since he insists that the prayers of exorcism be said in secret, he avoids the danger of causing the mental derangements that traditional rites of exorcism can produce. His kind of exorcism would correspond to Rahner's conception of it as nothing more than a prayer for aid against demonic affliction. As in all other such situations, no harm would be done if one has mistaken the nature of the trial from which one prays for deliverance.

One might think that, even though it is impossible to determine certainly when the devil is the source of a temptation, it would still be acceptable to stress the possibility or likelihood of diabolical temptation. However, apart from the dubious validity of the whole system of Christian demonology, emphasis on invisible spiritual tempters runs the same risk, though in a lesser degree, as the idea of diabolical possession. It could have pathological effects on a

[20] *The Imitation of Christ* 3, 15 (tr. A. Croft and H. Bolton, Milwaukee 1949) 114.
[21] Demal, *Pastoral Psychology* 46.

mentally unbalanced person, or, less damagingly, arouse groundless fears in sensitive consciences.

Pragmatically, it can be claimed that the theory of internal diabolical temptation has often helped to calm distressed persons. A certain kind of mentality is relieved when told that troublesome thoughts are not from itself but from the devil; for such a frame of mind the kind of reassurance offered by Robert Burton in the above passage from the *Anatomy of Melancholy* is very effective. Very likely, however, it would impede self-knowledge and the maturity that comes from accepting responsibility for one's own potentialities and tendencies.

Whatever the origin of temptations, one must resist them in the same way. St. Bernard of Clairvaux in the twelfth century made this point clear in a sermon on the discernment of spirits: He speaks of temptations that can come from the spirit of iniquity, that is, the prince of darkness, as well as from the spirit of the world and the spirit of the flesh; the two latter spirits (which he may mean simply as personifications of the world and the flesh) are satellites of the first. "Now then," he continues, "I do not think it is easy to be able to discern when our own spirit itself is speaking or when it listens to one of those other three spirits. But what difference does it make which one is speaking since they all say one and the same thing? What does it matter to know the person of the speaker when it is clear that what he speaks is pernicious? If it is the enemy, resist the enemy manfully. If it is your own spirit, refute it, and shed heartfelt tears that it has come into such misery and miserable servitude." [22]

Since the hypothesis of internal demonic temptation can result in the disorientations detailed above, and since the advantages claimed for it can be achieved in other ways, it could easily be discarded on the practical level, even by those who are not ready to eliminate demonology as a whole from the realm of theology. There is, in fact, a very considerable and increasing neglect of the devil, even within the comparatively conservative sphere of the religious orders, where many other traditional aspects of asceticism and devotion are faithfully retained. A recent analysis of temptation by a Jesuit priest in a journal for the members of such orders

[22] Bernard, Sermon 23 (*De discretione spirituum*) 3-4 (PL 183, 600-02).

omits all mention of the devil.[23] It can perhaps be taken as an example of the natural disinclination of educated Christians in the modern world to accept the demon-world of the past, even though many of them would no doubt feel constrained for doctrinal reasons to admit its existence. We will take up some of these doctrinal considerations in the next chapter.

[23] J. C. Futrell, "Temptation: A[ppetite] + R[ationalization] = S[urrender]," *Review for Religious* 19 (1960) 72-82.

VI
THE PRESENT STATUS
OF DEMONOLOGY

In the twenty centuries of Christianity much has passed for
Christian that is no longer accounted such. This is true of numerous concepts concerning evil spirits that were once felt to have
the sanction of divine revelation or the approval of ecclesiastical
authorities. But many demonological features still remain em-
bedded in the rituals, writings, and beliefs of Christians. This is
especially the case in large, doctrinally conservative bodies like the
Roman Catholic Church, but it is also true of smaller, more independent branches of Christendom like the Jehovah's Witnesses.
Although very critical of scriptural proofs advanced for doctrines
like the Trinity and the divine nature of Jesus, the Witnesses
nevertheless accept almost entirely the traditional post-biblical
alteration and systematization of scriptural demonology.

Catholic theologians, especially those educated in the scholastic
tradition, ordinarily determine the doctrinal status of a particular
teaching by weighing the various sources for the manifestation of
revealed truth within the Church. From their cumulative force they
decide the certainty, probability, or improbability of the teaching's
qualification as a dogma of faith.

This process, followed by seminary textbooks and manuals, has
greatly favored the concepts of Christian demonology we have
been studying. The existence of fallen angels, that is, of Satan and
the other evil demons, has been raised to the highest possible rank
as "a defined doctrine of divine and apostolic faith." Doctrines thus
designated are those that the theologians believe to have been in-
fallibly revealed as true and therefore unchangeable, and which
can be knowingly rejected by the Christian only at the risk of his
eternal salvation.

However, very little original theological thought has been expended upon the place of invisible spirits in the Christian religion since the scholastic syntheses of the Middle Ages. Most present-day theologians rely on these syntheses—especially that of St. Thomas—as a basis for vindicating the unassailable reality of angels and demons. In so doing they feel confident that they have an accurate idea of the precise nature of these creatures and the ways in which the possibility of demonic witchcraft, the rare but real occurrence of demonic possession, and the frequent instance of demonic temptation must be affirmed and explained.

Recently the validity of their arguments has been seriously questioned by the Dutch Jesuit theologian Peter Schoonenberg in the course of a discussion of evolution. We observe, he says, that, broadly speaking, higher forms of being always appear after the lower. Scholastic theology, however, could object that the existence of angels proves that there can be creatures that have no causal connection with our world:

> To this we could reply, first of all, that theology has not said the last word about angels and that it has in fact not even said the first word. The *existence* of personal created spirits does not follow apodictically from the mere fact that scripture mentions them in numerous places. This existence likewise is not absolutely guaranteed by the position they occupy in the liturgy and the doctrinal statements hitherto made by the Church. So far as scripture is concerned, as Karl Rahner explains in his articles "Angelologie" and "Dämonologie" (LTK 1,533-38; 3,145-47), scripture presupposes rather than affirms the existence of good and evil spirits. Regarding tradition, it is doubtful whether it adds anything in this matter to scripture. With respect to liturgical feasts, historical changes of the calendar of saints show that such feasts do not necessarily exclude the non-existence of their object. So far as doctrinal statements of the Church are concerned, for the Fourth Lateran Council (1215) the issue was not the existence and the creation of angels and devils, which the Albigensians themselves accepted. The crucial point, affirmed by the Council against the Albigensians, was that everything that exists has

been created by one God (ES 800). In other words, even this doctrinal statement, which most explicitly speaks of angels and devils, presupposes but does not directly affirm their existence.[1] For this reason, theologians should ask themselves whether they can claim without qualification that this existence is "de fide." One could object the encyclical *Humani generis* contains a warning against the doubt "whether angels are personal creatures" (ES 3891). The context, however, makes it unclear whether the denial is an "error" or merely contains "a danger of error."

Theologians should further ask themselves whether the existence of angels is a presupposition required by the content of other revealed truths or merely pertains to the world-view that served as a context in which these truths were revealed. Note, however, that even if angels and devils belong to this context, this fact does not prove that they do *not* exist.

All this should teach us to view revelation as a message of God's love for us and of salvation rather than as instructing us in the nature and kinds of beings existing in the whole of creation. What revelation tells us, in connection with good and evil spirits, about the dangers of sin and about God's willingness to come to our aid is more important than our knowledge concerning these spirits themselves.[2]

Schoonenberg is not convinced that the sources of revelation tell us even of the existence of intelligent creatures other than man. Therefore, he is not impressed with any data that theological and philosophical reflection upon these sources has produced in the past concerning the nature and activity of such creatures; nor does he seem hopeful that anything valuable on the subject will be forthcoming in the future.

It will be worthwhile to study in more detail each of the sources adduced and dismissed by Schoonenberg. In so doing we will be able to summarize some of the discussions of the previous chapters.

We may start with the encyclical letter *Humani generis,* issued in 1950, in which Pope Pius XII, while listing various theological

[1] Cf. A. Darlapp, "Dämon," LTK 3,142.
[2] P. Schoonenberg, *God's World in the Making* (Pittsburgh 1964) 8-9.

novelties that bear deadly fruit, declares that the question is being raised whether angels are personal beings. Schoonenberg points out that the context of this warning does not make it clear whether the Pope is actually condemning a definite error with these words or merely indicating the possibility of error. However, even if it could be established that he were definitely singling out this opinion as an error, it would be possible to hold that he was sounding a false alarm. In a recent address given at Rockhurst College in Kansas City, the Swiss theologian Hans Küng said: "It is the so-called ordinary magisterial documents of the Church which cause difficulties for Catholic theologians, rather than those relatively few to which Catholic theology applies the somewhat misleading predicate 'infallible.' How much does it actually take before a Catholic theologian admits that the particular fallible pronouncement like an encyclical or an address or a Roman decree was a mistake?" [3]

Among the examples of erroneous doctrinal decisions Küng cited were the condemnation of Galileo and the ban on reading the first three chapters of Genesis in the light of scientific insights. Both of these errors were the result of an over-literal interpretation of scripture; we must ask ourselves whether the scriptural bases of demonology are not founded upon the same kind of misreading.

The Galileo scandal was caused by the supposition that the scriptures supported the widespread opinion that the sun moved across the earth during the course of the day. The Church authorities of the time were willing to admit that the bible did not support this astronomical theory, if it could be proved scientifically erroneous; or, if it could not, they agreed that an opposite view could be held as an hypothesis. Galileo, unfortunately, wished to assert the Copernican view as a fact, even though his proofs were inadequate. The underlying assumption of his opponents was that the bible was a divine textbook that provided information on all aspects of creation or set a stamp of approval upon certain human conceptions of the universe and rejected others. The theory of evolution encountered the same difficulty as the Copernican theory of the solar system. Even though most churchmen in the nineteenth

[3] H. Küng, reported in the *National Catholic Reporter* 3, 1 (26 Oct. 1966) 1.

century were willing to admit that the structure and movement of the heavenly bodies fell outside the scope of divine revelation, they felt the circumstances of the world's origin and the beginning of human life were too closely connected to the purpose of revelation to be neglected by it and left to the fumblings of human reason.

Precisely the same objection is raised in the sphere of angelology and demonology. Though many theologians agree today that scripture contains no divine pronouncements on matters of natural science, they draw the line when it is a question of non-human intelligences. They feel that this area of reality is too important to have been excluded from heavenly illumination, and that when, for instance, Jesus is shown to speak in terms of the good and evil spirits evolved by the mythologies and folklore of the Jewish people, it would be unthinkable that there were in fact no such spirits, since countless numbers of people would be misled by his words into thinking that they did exist.

We may observe, first of all, that the vast majority of Christians who believed in evil spirits have not believed in the spirits as they are described in the bible but rather as they have been re-created by post-biblical speculation. Just as the scriptures were thought to verify a Ptolemaic view of a spherical earth surrounded by other spheres (whereas in fact they reflected the flat-world concepts of the Hebrews), so too it has been believed for centuries that the bible hinted of a great pre-cosmic sin of Lucifer and other angels, and that it described a war of hate against mankind by totally depraved unclean spirits and irredeemable principalities and powers, in a fashion nowhere verified in the texts.

Furthermore, like the claim for a geocentric universe, many of the tenets of demonology would be capable of a scientific demonstration, if they were true. If, for instance, demonic apparitions, wonders, and cases of possession could be properly witnessed and recorded they would no longer need to rely solely on faith. Unlike the theory of geocentricity, however, the belief in the existence of demons cannot be positively disproved. But its probability can be weakened in the face of an opposing theory—as was the case when the theory of the immediate creation of each species was confronted with the evidence for evolution. The theory of demonic possession, for instance, which is stated no more strongly in the bible than that of immediate creation, has been largely discredited by more sophisticated theories of illness. While there is still a possibility that it is valid, it could easily be discarded in practice if only the alleged necessity to believe it as a part of revelation could be removed.

Schoonenberg, as we saw, suggests that the existence of the angels and devils of the bible is not required by other revealed truths but "merely pertains to the world-view that served as a context in which these truths were revealed." There is no doubt that such invisible, or rather, usually invisible, creatures did belong to the world-view of biblical times. Many close parallels survive in contemporaneous literature, and even where there are none, it would be dangerous to assume that we have in such instances an item of divine revelation.

There is a close connection between the ancients' ideas of the spirit world and their concept of the heavenly bodies; it will not be out of place to point once more to the similarities between the claims made for demonology and those made for the Ptolemaic model of the universe. We have seen that the Jews and other ancient peoples often regarded the spirits in whom they believed as inhabitants of the heavens or spheres above the earth. These beliefs resemble present-day speculation about the existence of intelligent creatures in other worlds (and there are not lacking theologians to ponder over the place of such beings in the divine economy of salvation). The story of the angels who sinned with women and filled the earth with disaster and destruction, alluded to in the New Testament, is the same kind of story as H. G. Wells' account of an invasion from Mars. We might just as readily expect the divine revelation of such a science-fiction narrative as to assume that earlier legends of incursions from outer space were not fantasy but had a basis in the real world and were somehow revealed to their first retailers—whether their accounts originally appeared in scripture or not. In point of fact, the story in the *Book of Enoch* of the lustful angels and their fall was regarded by the early Fathers as divinely authenticated. But as the scriptural character of the *Book of Enoch* was impugned the story was replaced by another one, inspired by a part of Origen's great philosophical myth. It told of a fall of Lucifer and his angels before the fall of Adam. And though the scriptural bases of this tale are completely imaginary, it was, and is still, widely believed to have been sanctioned by the revealed word of God in the inspired scriptures.

We noted that many Catholic theologians attach a special significance to the personal nature of demons and other evil spirits in the bible because they are depicted as capable of thought and speech. It is noteworthy that certain theologians of other traditions find the primary religious meaning of the demonic in scripture not in its personal but precisely in its impersonal or antipersonal characteristics. Allan Galloway says that "it is when a man has descended to a sub-personal level of behavior, as for example in madness, that he is said to be possessed by demons." And he concludes that the demonic, "in expressing both the terror and the tempting fascination which man feels in the face of forces which are sub-personal in character yet superhuman in power, . . . represents essentially . . . the menace with which the impersonal structure of man's world threatens his personal life." [4]

Karl Rahner and Herbert Vorgrimler, who attempt to salvage the personal nature of demons, which they say is "laid down" by scripture and the magisterial statement of Pius XII in *Humani generis,* seem to reduce them to the human level by regarding them as "the powers *of* the world insofar as *this* world is a denial of God and a temptation to man." This view, they say, preserves the personal nature of demons, "since every essential disorder in the world is personally realized; it also preserves their plurality, which is to be visualized in the context of the world's qualitative and regional plurality." [5] Elsewhere they say: "Since the New Testament freely accepts the experiences of mankind and transmits them in purified form, we may take it that these principalities and powers are personal evil in the world as this is manifested in the various spheres and dimensions of human life, in self-will which leads to sin and death." [6] In this connection we may recall that in the purely historical narratives of the gospels the temptations and obstacles that Christ meets all proceed directly from human beings; the devil is not seen at work, but rather his presence is at times

---

[4] A. D. Galloway, *The Cosmic Christ* (New York 1951) 229. 231.
[5] Rahner and Vorgrimler, "Devils, Demons," *Theological Dictionary* (New York 1965) 126-27.
[6] *Ibid.* 379 ("Principalities and Powers").

extrapolated, as in Peter's denunciation of Ananias (Acts 5, 3), or in the figurative tableau (for such it seems to be) of the temptation of Jesus in the desert.

In the article on possession cited earlier, Rahner apparently upholds the traditional notion of diabolical illness. But the professorial obscurity of his language and his habit of retaining traditional terms for new concepts often make it extremely difficult to know what he really means. In the same article he states: "It is a truth of faith that preterhuman principalities and powers (devils) exist and are operative in the world," and refers to decrees of the Fourth Lateran Council and the Council of Trent.[7] Since he calls the principalities and powers evil and identifies them as devils and the agents of possession, he seems to accept the late patristic synthesis that fuses the various spirits of the bible into two groups of angels, the unchangeably good and the irrevocably depraved. Unlike Schoonenberg, he seems to believe that the Fourth Lateran Council declares this view to be unmistakably true.

Schoonenberg doubts that tradition—in the technical sense of a font of revelation—adds anything to the witness of scripture in the matter of the spirit world. At one time it was a common position among Catholic theologians that tradition could testify to a revealed truth that was not contained in scripture; but this view is becoming less widespread than the opinion that no truth is revealed in tradition that is not also contained in scripture. The patristic synthesis of angelology and demonology undoubtedly adds much to what is in scripture, but much of what it adds contradicts the scriptural assumptions and can hardly be raised to the dignity of revelation.

It is, however, beyond question that the Fourth Lateran Council, held in the first part of the thirteenth century, accepted the patristic views, since these views had become universal by the Middle Ages. The pertinent parts of the definition referred to by Schoonenberg, which is an expanded form of the creed, read as follows:

> Firmly we believe and we confess simply that the true God is one alone, eternal, immense, and unchangeable, incomprehensible, omnipotent, and ineffable, . . . creator of all visible and invisible things, of the spiritual and of the corporal; who

[7] *Ibid.* 365 ("Possession").

by his own omnipotent power at once from the beginning of time created each creature from nothing, spiritual, and corporal, namely, angelic and mundane, and finally the human, constituted, as it were, alike of the spirit and the body. For the devil and other demons were created by God good in nature, but they themselves through themselves have become wicked. But man sinned at the suggestion of the devil.

There is further mention of the devil after the redemptive work of Christ has been detailed; it is said that he will return to judge all men and allot to the wicked "everlasting punishment with the devil" and to the good "everlasting glory with Christ." [8]

In their article on "Devils," Rahner and Vorgrimler say that this definition "categorically declares that evil has not existed from the beginning but that everything evil has temporal limits and arises from the free choice of creatures. In this connection it is stated that God created Satan and the other devils good by nature but that they became evil of their own accord. Thus this definition presupposes the existence of devils." This is a far more accurate interpretation of the definition than the one in the same authors' article on "Possession," according to which the definition establishes the existence of devils as a truth of faith. To admit that an opinion is presupposed in a conciliar definition is to declare that it is not the object of the definition.

The existence of angels and demons was as much taken for granted by the fathers of the Lateran Council as the existence of men and the material world. The two latter categories of creatures were also said to be created by God, but no theologian has supposed that their existence was defined by the council. When the Lateran statement was repeated at the First Vatican Council in 1870 its only purpose was to describe God as the creator of all things (ES 3002). The question of the existence of the angels does not appear in the voluminous records of the discussions that preceded the approval of the definition, even though doubt on the point was widespread in the nineteenth century.

Furthermore, if it was not the intention of the Lateran Council to define the existence of the devil, it was certainly not its purpose to

[8] ES 800-01; tr. Roy J. Deferrari, *The Sources of Catholic Dogma* (St. Louis 1957) §§428-29.

define the traditional identification of the serpent with the devil, nor to assert as a truth of faith the eventual damnation of the devil. Once again, these notions are presuppositions that appear in the course of the council's assertion that no one is evil by nature and that punishment is meted out in payment for deliberately willed evil.

In the texts from the Council of Trent that Rahner and Vorgrimler cite in the "Possession" essay we again find only incidental mentions of the devil. Christians are warned of "the combat that yet remains with the flesh, with the world, with the devil"; and the sacrament of penance is described as "a remedy of life even to those who may afterwards [that is, after baptism] have delivered themselves to the servitude of sin, and to the power of Satan" (literally, "the demon's power"). The sacrament of extreme unction is described as a powerful defense at the end of life; "for, although *our adversary seeks* and seizes throughout our entire life occasions *to devour* (1 Pet. 5, 8) our souls in every manner, yet there is no time when he directs more earnestly all the strength of his cunning to ruin us completely, and if possible to drive us also from faith in the divine mercy, than when he sees that the end of life is upon us"; accordingly, by the help of this sacrament one "resists more easily the temptations of the evil spirit [lit. "of the demon"] who *lies in wait for his heel* (Gen. 3, 15)." [9]

These allusions to Satan in connection with the sacraments bring us to the last font cited by Schoonenberg, namely, the liturgy. He was most concerned about the feast days of angels that have found their way into the calendar of the saints, but more pertinent for demonology are the numerous prayers and ceremonies devised as aids against demonic attacks. Just as the ecclesiastical approval of festivals does not "necessarily exclude the non-existence of their object," so too the use of prayers against dangers does not exclude the possibility that the dangers envisaged were either totally different or totally imaginary. As civilization has advanced, many of these rituals have been eliminated from various reformed branches of Christendom, but in the larger groups the process of purification remains for the most part still to be accomplished.

[9] ES 1541. 1668. 1694. 1696 (*Sources* 806. 894. 907. 909).

After saying that devils were presupposed by the Lateran Council, Rahner and Vorgrimler (in "Devils") state that the meager data provided from this conciliar statement and the testimony of scripture "do not permit us to conceive of Satan (as popular piety often does) as an equal opponent of God, or to depict the character and doings of the devils. In view of the seriousness of saving history it would be untheological levity to look on Satan and his devils as a sort of 'hobgoblins knocking about the world.' " They go on to characterize devils as the powers of this world, which, as we saw above, could be interpreted to mean nothing more than the disorders that men bring upon themselves.

We must conclude that a great deal of the demonology evolved under the name of Christian teaching can only be characterized as "untheological levity." The representations of the spirit world in scripture betray signs of simple folkloristic origin, and the modifications that these images and myths underwent when they came into contact with later cultures and philosophies are no longer convincing, however satisfying they may have been for past ages. A continued adherence to these views, as if they constituted an essential part of divine revelation, runs the risk of exposing the whole Christian mission to ridicule.

It is certain that in the past the attribution of misfortune to invisible creatures at enmity with mankind has often radically hindered the proper diagnosis and treatment of the ills that afflict the human race. This has been the case not only in the obvious examples of witch persecution and possession manias, but also in less sensational circumstances where a vague dread of intangible adversaries has distracted attention from applying remedies to tangible causes and effects.

Although it is possible that evil spirits exist, at the present time it does not seem probable; but whether or not they exist, it does not appear to be necessary to believe in them in order to cope with the problems of human life. Given the evils that belief in demonology has caused in the past, and given also the uncertainty of its claim to a place in Christian revelation and theology, it would seem best to act as though evil spirits did not exist, until such time as their existence is forced upon us.

INDEX

I. SCRIPTURE REFERENCES

Note: All references follow the numbering of the Revised Standard Version

II. GENERAL REFERENCES